Changemakers! Practitioners Advance Equity and Access in Out-of-School Time Programs

A Volume in:
Current Issues in Out-of-School Time

Series Editor

Helen Janc Malone

Current Issues in Out-of-School Time

Series Editor

Helen Janc Malone
Institute for Educational Leadership

*Social and Emotional Learning in Out-Of-School Time:
Foundations and Futures* (2018)
Elizabeth Devaney & Deborah A. Moroney

The Growing Out-of-School Time Field: Past, Present, and Future (2017)
Helen Janc Malone & Tara Donahue

Current Issues in Out-of-School Time Book Series Boards

Changemakers! Practitioners Advance Equity and Access in Out-of-School Time Programs

Edited by

Sara Hill
Femi Vance

INFORMATION AGE PUBLISHING, INC.
Charlotte, NC • www.infoagepub.com

Library of Congress Cataloging-In-Publication Data

Names: Hill, Sara, editor. | Vance, Femi, editor.
Title: Changemakers! : practitioners advance equity and access in
  out-of-school time programs / edited by Sara Hill, Femi Vance.
Other titles: Changemakers! (Information Age Publishing)
Description: Charlotte, NC : Information Age Publishing, Inc. 2019. |
  Series: Current issues in out-of-school time | Includes bibliographical
  references. | Summary: "A foundational tenet of the Out-of-School Time
  (OST) field is that all youth deserve impactful and engaging learning
  experiences. That requires that organizations, programs, and OST
  professionals remain responsive to the emerging needs of their diverse
  youth population and the communities in which they live. This book
  illustrates the tensions that arise when organizations and OST
  professionals try to engage all youth, especially the underserved - when
  infrastructure, funding, and mindsets have not kept pace with the
  evolving needs of youth and their communities. The issues raised in this
  book - funding, outreach, engagement of immigrant families - have yet to
  be fully explored with an equity lens. Within these broad topics, this
  book will bring to the surface the equity and access challenges as well
  as posit solutions and strategies. Each chapter is written from an
  insider's perspective, by practitioners themselves, who articulate some
  of the key, and relevant issues in the field. Each chapter ends with a
  Research-Practice Connection section written by the editors, which
  discusses the topic from a research lens, and generates a set of
  questions that can be used by researchers in future studies to explore
  the topic in a more in-depth, and expansive manner"-- Provided by
  publisher.
Identifiers: LCCN 2019008651 (print) | LCCN 2019980403 (ebook) | ISBN
  9781641136204 (paperback) | ISBN 9781641136211 (hardcover) | ISBN
  9781641136228 (ebook)
Subjects: LCSH: After-school programs--Social aspects--United States. |
  Children with social disabilities--Education--United States. |
  Educational equalization--United States. | Community and school--United
  States. | Out-of-school programs.
Classification: LCC LC34.4 .C53 2019 (print) | LCC LC34.4 (ebook) | DDC
  371.04--dc23
LC record available at https://lccn.loc.gov/2019008651
LC ebook record available at https://lccn.loc.gov/2019980403

Printed in the United States of America

CONTENTS

PART III

EQUITY THROUGH CRITICAL PRACTICE

PART IV

SUMMARY AND CONCLUSION

ENDORSEMENTS

This is the book the OST field needs now. A critical read for anyone in youth development or OST, the authors push all of us, youth workers, organizational leaders, funders, policy makers, and researchers to think critically about both the structures and practices of OST programs in relation to the systemic inequities that exist in our country. Skillfully linking examples from the OST field with evidence and theory from scholarship on youth development, the chapters spark readers to think about our own work in new ways. More importantly, the book offers an opportunity for all of us, whatever our role in the field, to intentionally engage OST programs as a tool for dismantling inequity. I will be thinking about how to apply the lessons from this book long after I have closed its cover for the first, but decidedly not last, time.

— Nancy L. Deutsch
Professor, Curry School of Education, University of Virginia

With a resurgence of dialogue about the role of the out-of-school time (OST) field in educational, economic and racial equity, this book provides timely and useful strategies for practitioners, capacity builders, policymakers and funders. Hill and Vance unveil a refreshingly bold call to action through practical experiences and research. The writers bring to life the continuous and deep personal exploration that is required of individuals at all levels to disrupt structural oppression and courageously challenge the field to shine a light on how the youth development field perpetuates oppressive dominant culture norms. From exploring the imbalance of power between schools and

OST programs to the role of philanthropy in the fueling a toxic system to fostering brave, trauma informed spaces for youth to explore their identity to elevating professional development that normalizes the exploration of power, privilege and oppression – this book covers a broad range of needs and solutions that advance equity in the OST field toward a more just society. I'm encouraged by the discourse that will be sparked by this publication and am hopeful that counter-dominant and equity-driven investments, policies and practices will become the new norm across all levels of the OST ecosystem.

— Ruth Obel-Jorgensen
California School-Age Consortium

Changemakers! Practitioners Advance Equity and Access in Out-of-School Time Programs offers an uplifting and inspiring blend of narrative, scholarship, and human experience focused on issues of access and equity in the out-of-school time field. Believing that there is a pathway to change before us, the authors have carefully crafted chapters of essential guidance for out-of-school time program directors, leaders, researchers, and funders towards transforming our field to fairly and fully meet the needs of and support all children and youth. An invaluable resource of practical and on-the-ground information.

— Georgia Hall
Director and Sr. Research Scientist,
National Institute on Out-of-School Time
Associate Director
Wellesley Centers for Women
Managing Editor
Afterschool Matters
Wellesley College

PREFACE

CHANGEMAKERS!

Practitioners Advance Equity and Access in Out-of-School Time Programs

Sarah Zeller-Berkman

I was six years old when my dad first went to prison. His arrest was related to some of the radical movements in which he was involved in the 1970s and 1980s. His second, longer stint in prison started when I was nine and lasted until I was 16. When I returned home from college at twenty-one, I started volunteering in a program for pre-teens and teens who were experiencing parental incarceration. At twenty-three, I had the privilege to run my own teen program for youth whose mothers were incarcerated at Taconic Prison through the nonprofit Hour Children. We had an amazing group of young people, caretakers, and volunteers. We made prison visits fun and did lots of other trips on weekends. We all did our best to assist the overworked caretakers in navigating the systems—getting the kids in their care into good schools (which seemed few and far between), accessing mental health services for children experiencing multiple traumas (also few and far between), and arguing for basic supports from degrading and bureaucratic systems. I often felt like all I was doing was helping to keep people's heads above water in the face of policies, practices, and carceral systems that needed major change.

Changemakers! Practitioners Advance Equity and Access in Out-of-School Time Programs,
pages ix–xi.

Changemakers! Practitioners Advance Equity and Access in Out-of-School Time Programs is a book I needed back then. It offers tools for supporting young people and a roadmap to changing unjust systems. Pushing the field of out-of-school time towards changing organizations and institutions as opposed to just changing young people has a legacy that can be traced to the youth rights movements of the early 1960s. The youth participation movement, like other groups such as people of color, women, LGBT people, and Native peoples emerged from the 1960s poised to advocate for greater control over issues that impacted their lives. Much of the early writing in the field of youth development came out of the National Commission on Resources for Youth (NCRY). NCRY was established in 1967 to foster more active and significant social roles for young people or "youth participation." Throughout the 1970s and early 1980s the NCRY published literature that explored and extolled the benefits of youth participation for young people, communities, and institutions.

Scholars like Dollar (1975), Coleman (1974), and Costin (1982) highlighted the ways that youth are positioned as a low power group in this society and recommended institutional change at the federal and local level to encourage youth participation to foster connections between young people and others. The aforementioned scholars of this time also pushed back against the idea of adolescents as "not yet" people in need of development, believing that it alienated youth. The youth development work in this period of time was about transforming societies' relationship to young people. Even recommendations emerging from large government agencies like the commerce department (NTIS, 1971) and Office of Juvenile Justice and Delinquency Prevention (1980) focused on youth advocacy. One of the major themes of the program was youth involvement, defined as "meaningful youth participation in policy decisions affecting youth for the purpose of better defining youth needs and impacting on the practices, policies and utilization of funds in youth serving institutions." As a whole, the scholars during the 60s, 70s and 80s were pushing to partner with youth to change the civic ecosystem in which young people lived. They wanted youth to be the drivers of institutional and systemic change (Zeller-Berkman, 2011).

In my current role as an Academic Director of a Youth Studies Master's program, I see this book as required reading for the next generation of practitioner-scholars interested in promoting a revolutionary approach to youth development. This book is an important reminder of the field of out-of-school time's potential to promote a more equitable future for and with **all** young people. The authors highlighted in this book are at the forefront of a movement to ensure young people have access to high quality programming, the resources they need and the respect they deserve. The authors acknowledge that there must be concerted effort to provide for young people who have been consistently under-resourced and/or actively oppressed. This may require retraining staff and altering supports and structures to enable marginalized youth to thrive. The authors in this book have no desire to fit youth into situations that are not working for them, but rather to partner with young people to transform inequitable organizations and institutions to better serve them.

Changemakers! Practitioners Advance Equity and Access in Out-of-School Time Programs reframes problematic narratives in our field while giving concrete strategies that promote multiple levels of change. The practitioner-scholars highlighted in this book challenge readers to focus change efforts on transforming not just young people, but the adults that work with youth at the point-of-service as well as implementing institutional and systemic change. Recognizing that our myopic focus on changing young people, not unjust systems, perpetuates the notion that youth are empty vessels to be filled, not partners in the struggle for social justice (Zeller-Berkman, 2010). The editors of *Changemakers! Practitioners Advance Equity and Access in Out-of-School Time Programs* have strategically aligned research and practice on what works to promote equity and access with the practitioner positioned as expert. Hill and Vance issue a call to action that encourages researchers and practitioners to band together to interrogate these critical issues while leaving the reader with questions and an invitation to take the work further. I stand ready to partner with others who work the hyphens of activist-practitioner-scholars to answer this call to action.

REFERENCES

Dollar, B. (1975). *Youth participation: A concept paper.* A Report to the Department of Health, Education and Welfare, Offices of Youth Development prepared by the National Commission on Resources for Youth. New York, NY: National Commission on Resources for Youth.

Coleman, J. (1974). Panel on youth of the president's science advisory committee. *Youth: Transition to adulthood.* Chicago, IL: University of Chicago Press.

Costin (1982). *Youth participation in youth advocacy: A practical guide for developing programs.* Prepared for the U.S. Office of Juvenile Justice and Delinquency Prevention by the National Commission on Resources for Youth.

Zeller-Berkman, S. (2010, Autumn). Critical development? Using a critical theory lens to examine the current role of evaluation in the youth development field. New directions for evaluation. *Special Issue: Critical Social Theory and Evaluation Practice, 2010* (127), 35–44.

Zeller-Berkman, S. (2011). *"So what I got a mouth!" Reclaiming attachment and active citizenship through adult-youth partnerships.* (Doctoral dissertation). Retrieved on Oct 5, 2018 from ProQuest LLC (3460280)

DEDICATIONS

We dedicate this volume to the skilled youth development professionals that navigate complex equity and access issues on a daily basis and still continue to positively impact the lives of youth and families. Thank you for the commitment, dedication, and love that you show to our youth.

Dedicated to the American Educational Research Association Out-of-School Time Special Interest Group.

PART I

INTRODUCTION

INTRODUCTION

Sara Hill and Femi Vance

A tenet of the out-of-school time (OST)[1] field is that all youth deserve impactful and engaging learning experiences. Organizations, programs, and professionals must be responsive to the existing and emerging needs of the increasingly diverse[2] children and youth[3] that they serve and the communities in which they live. To that end, this book focuses primarily on equity and access in the OST context because while access is on the increase, the field has yet to meet the needs of the most underserved communities (Afterschool Alliance, 2014; Dawes, 2018).

Equity and access are terms that get used too often without definition. Throughout this book, we use equity to mean when young people have the tools, resources, and other supports they need to achieve desired outcomes such as self-sufficiency and well-being. Equity is often confused with equality, where everyone receives the same resources; however, a cookie-cutter set of resources is unlikely to meet

[1] Out-of-school time (OST) is the term used in this book for programs for children and youth which takes place during the non-school hours. This can include before and after school as well as during school breaks (e.g. summer). OST Programs can take place in school buildings as well as stand-alone community based organizations or other non-school contexts, such as museums.

[2] By the term "diverse," we mean those who have been marginalized by mainstream institutions including ethnic and racial minorities, GLBTQ individuals, and those with disabilities, among others.

[3] By the terms "children" and "youth" we mean primarily school-age youth, e.g. grades K–12.

Changemakers! Practitioners Advance Equity and Access in Out-of-School Time Programs,
pages 3–10.
Copyright © 2019 by Information Age Publishing

3

the needs of all youth. Rather, equity is the set of resources that helps to meet the unique needs of each young person.

Access, in this book, refers to ensuring that OST programs are available in all communities and that youth and their families know about them. Access also means that OST programs provide structures to help youth and families enroll and, once enrolled, provide ongoing supports so that they continue to participate and thrive.

We selected the chapters for this book because they represent either typical or unique aspects of equity and access as defined above. Taken together, the chapters illustrate and explore the tensions that arise when organizations and OST professionals try to engage all youth—especially the under-resourced and underserved—when infrastructure, funding, and mindsets have not kept pace with the evolving needs of youth and their communities. We encouraged the authors in *Changemakers!* to articulate the issues from the perspective of on-the-ground youth development professionals, and to provide some solutions that have worked in their own context which might provide guidance for others struggling with the same issues.

OVERVIEW OF CHAPTERS

Access to afterschool programs, primarily in under-resourced neighborhoods serving communities of color, is still problematic. In a survey conducted in 2013, "more than 4.1 million, or 61 percent, of African-American parents and 4.2 million, or almost half, of Latino parents of children who are not enrolled in an afterschool program say that they would enroll their children in quality afterschool programs if one were available—significantly higher than the national average of 38 percent" (Afterschool Alliance, 2013, p. 7). While participation is on an upward trajectory (Afterschool Alliance, 2014), there are troubling differences in access. The "demand for afterschool programs are much higher among children from low-income households compared to higher-income households, as well as higher among African-American and Hispanic children than Caucasian children" (Afterschool Alliance, 2014, p. 9). We have yet to engage in research that helps to understand the complex barriers to access, and "equity and access issues continue to bedevil the field" (Grantmakers for Education, 2014).

Dawes (2018) mentions several obstacles in her review of access to OST programs including the lack of family involvement and the lack of programs that target young men of color. Some of the intentional strategies she articulates in her review are explored in this book in depth (see chapter by Gilgoff). However, the authors in this book further the discussion of equity and access by identifying additional obstacles. They include structures such as institutional bias and racism (see chapter by Sharpe), ways that funders create roadblocks through the grants process (see chapter by Fabiano) as well as programmatic structures such as outreach and onboarding procedures that can stymie access (see chapter by Loeper).

This book sheds light on these additional obstacles, and provides suggestions and recommendations grounded in practice.

Quality is the other side of the equity equation, and it's important to note that in the paragraph above, parents say that they would enroll their children in *quality* programs. Equity and quality must go hand in hand. There is a general consensus of what quality in OST programs looks like (Grantmakers for Education, 2014), as well as consensus on what quality relationships look like (Akiva et al., 2016). However, quality can certainly be viewed at a deeper level, beyond just "relationships, active learning, inquiry-based approaches, and choice" (Funders for Education, 2014). For example, how are we changing the culture of our organizations at all levels to recognize and address implicit bias (see chapter by Sharpe)? How are we preparing staff to engage with young people and families who are experiencing trauma and stress (see chapter by McGee, Loeper)? How are we preparing youth to deal with racist institutions of higher education after we've prepared them academically through our OST programs for college attendance (McGee)? How are we creating programs that are inclusive of youth with disabilities (see chapter by Stolz)? This book also intends to address some of these deeper questions regarding program quality.

ORGANIZATION OF BOOK

We organized the book into two sections. The first section, *Shaping Organizations for Access and Equity* examines how organizational policies can set the stage to position OST programs to either thwart or create quality programs for all youth. The second section, *Advancing Equity through Critical Practice,* explores how OST professionals can address equity and access while working directly with youth. These two sections reflect two facets of OST: 1) the structures, including policy and procedures, embedded in organizations and programs that either perpetuate or dismantle inequity and lack of access (Vandell et al., 2004); and 2) point-of-service quality (Smith & Hohmann, 2005), which emphasizes the importance of staff, their relationships with youth, and the activities that they design and implement. Organizational structure and point-of-service quality work together to provide youth with enriching experiences. This means that equity and access must be addressed simultaneously with these two aspects in mind.

Shaping Organizations for Access and Equity

This section is well suited for OST professionals who manage one or more programs. The chapter topics—partnerships, outreach, funding, organizational policy, access for disabled youth—generally fall into their responsibilities and purview. It is also valuable for other OST professionals who must articulate these issues and advocate for equity and access within their organizations.

Organizational Policy. As the demographic makeup of the US undergoes a sea change of diversification, many nationwide historical legacy youth development organizations are facing a critical question: What will it take for us to stay relevant in the 21st Century? We must work for equity, and achieving equity requires us to address root issues such as equalizing the balance of power, access to programs and opportunity, allocation of resources, and decision-making power in youth-serving organizations. In the opening chapter, *Putting Our Minds to It: Implicit Bias and Advancing Equity in Youth Development*, Kathryn Sharpe lays out the structural issues that organizations face, as well as multiple avenues for organizational transformation. She explores strategies for mitigating implicit bias at the organizational policy level as well as the individual staff/volunteer level and shares methods for spearheading change from the leadership level, from the grassroots, and from a more collective approach. The goal of this chapter is for every youth development professional to see a role that (s)he can play in their own organization's transformation.

Equitable Partnerships. Increasingly, state, federal, and philanthropic funding requires school and afterschool programs to collaborate on new educational initiatives. In Chapter 2, *On the Level: Local Networks Creating Deeper and More Equitable School-Community Partnerships*, Ken Anthony provides the rationale for and practical strategies to achieve more equitable partnerships between two important actors in the OST context, schools and afterschool programs. Meaningful, effective partnerships require school leadership and afterschool program staff to intentionally build their capacity for collaboration. However, an imbalance of power between schools and afterschool programs has a negative impact on programs—creating situations where there is limited resource-sharing and a lack of formal communication structures. This has an impact on young people's learning and can lead to substantial misalignment of the goals, beliefs, and pedagogy between school and afterschool programs. This chapter uses The Coalition for New Britain's Youth school-afterschool partnership as a case study to explore potential strategies to mitigate the power imbalance and develop successful partnerships. This chapter also illustrates what partnerships look like on the ground and provides valuable resources for practitioners wanting to improve their own school-community partnerships.

Outreach and Retention. In Chapter 3, *Extending a Mighty Hand: Outreach and Retention Strategies to Help Our Least Supported Youth,* Rachel Loeper provides several suggestions and strategies to attract youth to programs and retain them. Practitioners and organizations in urban environments too often miss the point of their mission. Teaching artists and youth development group leaders and facilitators develop high-quality programs but fail to adequately match them to their intended audience. They often overlook the students who need services most in favor of more well-supported youth. As a result, urban areas are inundated with "quality" programming that may not speak to the youth living in the neighborhood. Even worse, the topic or programming is on-point, but families and youth don't know about it. Outreach and retention aren't as sexy as program development, however, without strong outreach and retention practices, nonprofit organizations cannot fulfill their service missions. This chapter makes the case that organizations need to be attuned to the audience for their programs.

Funding. Current funding structures keep nonprofits operating in a crisis mode, and with a poverty and scarcity mentality; forcing organizations to compete instead of collaborating. In addition, Request for Proposals (RFPs), by their design, require applicants to describe children and youth from a pathological, deficit model. Funders often give small sums and short timeframes to "fix" the problems. In Chapter 4, *Rooted in Scarcity and Deficit: Time to Reconsider the Funding Process,* Rebecca Fabiano describes from a youth development professional's perspective, what it's like to apply for a grant, and how the current funding models make it challenging to do the meaningful work with youth who may have experienced trauma, and in communities that have been chronically under-resourced and underrepresented. The chapter ends with suggestions for funders related to updating the language in RFPs to reflect an asset-based viewpoint of youth and communities and to developing outcomes that are more aligned with positive youth development and building healthy, sustainable communities.

Access for Disabled youth. Disabled youth should have the same access to quality OST programs as other youth. Even though the Americans with Disabilities Act (ADA) requires programs to provide accommodations that support disabled youths' involvement, a lack of programming limits disabled youths' options and often does not appeal to their strengths and interests. Despite violations to the ADA and a history of disability segregation, many youth program leaders and parents are advocating for disability access in OST programs. While integrated programs are mandated by law, some families still opt for segregated programs that have typically been more responsive to the disability-specific needs of their children and give families a "reprieve" from the constant need to advocate for their child. In Chapter 5, *What Does it Take to Provide Disabled Youth Access to Out-of-School Time Programs?* Suzanne Stolz shares her experiences with various programs and explores the perspectives of parents, youth, and OST providers in relation to how disability access is navigated in the field. She outlines the basic legal requirements of the ADA in relation to OST programs, discusses the benefits and drawbacks of integrated and segregated programs, and describes what it takes to provide a strong inclusive program.

Equity Through Critical Practice

Working alongside young people is at the heart of the OST field. The chapters in this section will speak to current, former, and aspiring OST professionals as well as those who must shape the environment in which learning opportunities take place. The authors in this section highlight the primacy of youth developing a critical perspective, emphasize the need to build on young people's skills and current resources, and remind us that, for our most vulnerable youth, advocating for equity is a marathon, not a sprint.

Critical Youth Development. In Chapter 6, *Critical Youth Development: Living and Learning at the Intersections of Life,* Merle McGee writes a powerful description of an approach to youth development that engages youth in identity exploration and social/political education. Traditional youth development focuses on young people's social, ethical, emotional, physical, artistic, and cognitive competencies. Youth development practitioners have offered important approaches to building life skills, personal agency, and resiliency that can reduce risky behaviors and promote future planning. However, youth workers operate in a world where racialized trauma and gender inequities uniquely impact our youth's life options. For both youth at the margins and those with social and cultural privilege, the ability to navigate discussions around identity, power, privilege and oppression will be a key life and leadership competency.

Working with Boys and Young Men of Color. In Chapter 7, *Maintaining Momentum to Empower Boys and Young Men of Color in the Out-of-School-Time Field,* Jon Gilgoff shares how to continue the Boys and Young Men of Color movement by institutionalizing related practices, policies, and procedures. In recent years, efforts to empower boys and young men of color have grown with the recognition that this group is disproportionately impacted by numerous stressors, resulting in adverse health, education, employment, and overall life outcomes. Male youth of color are overrepresented in special education, school discipline, and under-represented in graduating classes and college enrollment. They are exposed to criminal justice at levels far beyond other demographic groups and are injured or die from violence at alarming rates. While the OST field has been serving marginalized males throughout its history, over the last decade there has been a marked increase in efforts to address this need and affect change. Jon Gilgoff thoughtfully reflects on progress made and the work still left to be done.

Museums, out-of-school time, and The Immigrant Community. Many OST programs understand the value of engaging families, however, many programs struggle to do so well. This is especially true for programs that serve immigrant families who may be unaware of what OST programs in the United States can offer or how OST programs operate. In the final chapter, *NYSCI Neighbors: Engaging Immigrant Families in Out-of-School Time Experiences,* Andrés Henriquez and Sonia Bueno illustrate that engaging immigrant youth and families requires intentionality and a strong commitment to understanding the varied perspectives, experiences, and needs of this population. The authors describe the New York Hall of Science's unique, whole-family approach to closing the opportunity gap that exists for immigrant youth who may excel in science, technology, engineering, and math fields (STEM). They offer best practices for inviting families to partner with OST programs so that together, they can support children's educational aspirations.

LIMITATIONS

When we were looking for chapters for this book we cast a wide net hoping for authors who could address some of the critical issues in the field in the areas of access and equity. We selected what we considered to be the best of the submissions. We feel our book is making a valuable contribution to the discussion and exploration of obstacles to access and equity, however, we have certainly not covered the gamut. We still need explorations of other types of obstacles to access and equity and strategies to overcome them in a range of areas, for example, GLBTQ children and youth, rural youth, and youth in foster care, among others.

Even though we have not covered the complete range of settings and demographic features, there are intersectionalities in access and equity which can be applied no matter the dimension. For example, the exploration of bias in national "legacy" organizations (chapter by Sharpe) includes a wide range of settings, including rural ones. The topics of funding (see chapter by Fabiano) as well as building networks across institutions (see chapter by Anthony) apply to most, if not all, OST contexts. Issues of race, identity, and gender (see Chapters by McGee and Gilgoff) are relevant to nearly all settings and geographic locations.

TOGETHER, WE ARE STRONGER

Equity and access in OST programs are paramount to the success of all youth. To realize our vision of widely available, high-quality OST programs that dismantle inequity, researchers and practitioners must band together. Only then will we consistently apply innovative strategies and research-informed methods to make progress. We consider this book to be a first step. All of the chapters intentionally assume an insider posture; they are a collection of pieces written from the point of view of experienced practitioners in OST programs and intermediary organizations[4] and each chapter ends with a "Research Connections Written By Editors" section, that advances a set of questions for researchers to explore the topic in the future, in a more in-depth, and expansive, manner.

REFERENCES

Afterschool Alliance (2013, July). *The importance of afterschool and summer learning programs in African-American and Latino communities* (Issue Brief No. 59). Retrieved from https://afterschoolalliance.org/documents/issue_briefs/issue_African-American-Latino-Communities_59.pdf

Afterschool Alliance. (2014). *America after 3pm.* Washington, DC. Retrieved from http://www.afterschoolalliance.org/AA3_Full_Report.pdf.

Akiva, T., Li, J., Martin, K. M., *Horner, C. G., *McNamara, A. R. (2016). *Simple Interactions: Piloting a strengths- and interactions-based professional development inter-*

---

[4] Intermediaries are nonprofits set up to provide professional development and capacity building for other nonprofits and their staff.

vention for out-of-school time programs. Child & Youth Care Forum. doi:10.1007/s10566-016-9375-9

Dawes, N. (2018). Access to out-of-school time programs for underserved youth. In H. Jane Malone & T. Donahue (Eds.), *The growing out-of-school time field: Past, present and future* (pp. 47–70).Charlotte, NC: Information Age Publishing.

Grantmakers for Education (2014). *Grantmakers and thought leaders on out-of-school: Survey & interview report*. Portland, OR: Author.

Smith, C., & Hohman, C. (2005). *Full findings from the youth PQA validation study*. Ypsilanti, MI: High Scope. Retrieved from http://cypq.org/sites/cypq.org/files/publications/YPQA%20Full%20Findings%20Val%20Study%2005.pdf.

Vandell, D. L., Reisner, E. R., Brown, B. B., Pierce, K. M., Dadisman, K., & Pechman, E. M. (2004). *The study of promising after-school programs: Descriptive report of the promising programs*. Madison, WI: University of Wisconsin, Madison, Wisconsin Center for Education Research. Retrieved from http://childcare.wceruw.org/pdf/pp/study_of_after_school_activities_descriptive_report_year1.pdf.

PART II

SHAPING ORGANIZATIONS FOR ACCESS AND EQUITY

CHAPTER 1

PUTTING OUR MINDS TO IT

Implicit Bias and Advancing
Equity in Youth Development

Kathryn Sharpe

Two Somali young women stand backstage waiting to perform a dramatic piece in the arts competition at the State Fair. They nervously peer out at the audience seated in front of the stage—mostly white, many wearing John Deere caps or waving fans in the sweltering heat. The young women practice the lines for their skit about the experience of wearing a headscarf. When their names are called, they take a deep breath, smile widely, and step onto stage, the new face of 4-H. In an organization historically known for white rural farm kids showing their cows at the State Fair, these young women are part of the organization's evolution to engage today's diverse youth in new ways, thereby transforming not only its demographics but also its way of doing business.

All over the U.S., similar scenes are playing out in other long-standing youth development programs. The demographics of the nation's population are shifting and estimates predict that it will be become a "majority-minority" nation in 2044, meaning that non-Hispanic whites will become less than 50% of the population (Colby & Ortman, 2015). This change is occurring more quickly among youth. In 2014, students of color became the majority in America's public schools

Changemakers! Practitioners Advance Equity and Access in Out-of-School Time Programs,
pages 13–28.
Copyright © 2019 by Information Age Publishing

13

(Carr, 2016). As the U.S. youth population becomes more racially and ethnically diverse, we are also witnessing an increase in diversity in terms of religion, nationality, immigration status, sexual orientation and gender identity, as well as the range of physical and mental abilities. Diversification goes beyond mere issues of identity, because these youth also experience significant economic disparities, among others, that exist throughout our society between majority members and marginalized[1] members of the population (Carr, 2016).

The youth population described above differs dramatically from the one that many youth development organizations were originally established to serve, especially the ones I call "legacy" youth development organizations; those in existence for more than 100 years and which reach thousands of youth across the nation. 4-H, YMCA, YWCA, Girl Scouts, and Boy Scouts are a few of the most prominent. As the demographic makeup of the US undergoes a sea change, legacy organizations are facing critical questions such as, "Who are we in the 21st century?" "Whom will we serve in 20 years, and how will we do it?" "How will we ensure that all youth benefit from positive youth development experiences that help them thrive?"

Legacy organizations' policies and practices reflect the dominant culture's values and beliefs; those of white middle class families. If legacy organizations want to engage authentically with youth from different backgrounds and cultures, they must wrestle with their own institutional racism and other kinds of systemic discrimination. This requires organizations to realize that diversity and equity are not synonymous, and that simply seeking to increase their organization's diversity is not enough. In a society with dramatic disparities, they must address equity at a deeper level, which will require legacy organizations to change how decisions are made and resources allocated, beyond just shifting the demographics of their participants and staff. For legacy youth development organizations to stay relevant in the 21st century and engage in best practices for quality youth development, they must commit to creating equity in their organization and their organization's policies and procedures.

POSITIONING MYSELF

I have worked for nearly 10 years at the University of Minnesota Extension Center for Youth Development with the 4-H program, so I am part of a legacy youth development organization. A major focus of my work with 4-H has been to develop outreach strategies to engage traditionally underserved communities, cultivate new youth and families, recruit and train more diverse volunteers, and establish partnerships with organizations serving these communities. As a White, US-born,

---

[1] I use the term "marginalized" as Russell & Van Campen: (2011): "to denote the ways that some young people are pushed to the margins; that emphasizes the social processes that render youth marginal, rather than focusing on deficits based in the person (i.e. defining youth as 'at risk' or 'vulnerable')."

middle-class, cisgender[2] woman who is highly educated, this work has made me aware of the critical importance of self-reflection about my own privilege and to employ strategies to manage it. I have found important tools and strategies for mitigating my implicit bias, or unexamined judgements, from reading new research. As my own organization pivots our internal culture to engage traditionally underserved audiences and create more equitable conditions, I see how my personal process parallels that of 4-H, a historically majority-dominated organization, and of my colleagues within it.

In this chapter, I argue that in order to engage in quality youth development in the 21st century, legacy organizations need to embrace an equity framework to transform their policies and programs. Because organizations have been shaped by serving youth primarily from the dominant culture, they must address the implicit biases embedded in their organizational culture. They also need to do so at the personal level with themselves, their staff, and volunteers. This chapter will explore the process of organizational change, both from a top-down and a bottom-up approach. I introduce some common implicit biases and offer strategies for mitigating them in an effort to advance equity in legacy organizations.

The role of legacy organizations in advancing equity is especially important because of the significant impact they have given their size and level of influence in the youth development field. For example, 4-H, Girl Scouts, and Boy Scouts combined serve over 10 million young people each year in the U. S. (National 4-H Council, 2017; Girl Scouts of the USA, 2017; Boy Scouts of America, 2016). Because of their broad range of participants they are well positioned to bring together youth from the dominant culture and marginalized young people to build much-needed societal interconnectedness.

For this chapter, I interviewed four leaders from legacy organizations who have invested significant work into advancing equity. I refer to them using the pseudonyms "Michael," "Teresa," "Josephine," and "Mario." All are people of color with administrative-level leadership positions within prominent legacy organizations serving urban, suburban, and rural populations in the Upper Midwest. Some have experience on the East and West Coasts. Each has led efforts to advance diversity and equity within their organizations. Through my interviews with each of them, I garnered important information on their paths as organizational leaders. I have also drawn upon my own experience as a front–line youth worker, and now mid-level manager, engaged in organizational change and personal as well as interpersonal transformation.[3]

---

[2] Cisgender denotes or relates to a person whose sense of personal identity and gender corresponds with their birth sex.

[3] Interpersonal transformation in this context means working to help people address and transform their own biases and the ways they relate to others.

History of Legacy Institutions

Legacy organizations have a long tradition of serving the majority population: white, middle class, heterosexual, and United States-born. It is ironic that many legacy organizations were historically created to reach out to marginalized young people a century ago, such as isolated rural children, immigrant families or low-income youth living in urban tenements (Russell & Van Campen, 2011).

The original goals of these organizations were to assimilate youth into the norms (language, values, practices, etc.) of the dominant culture, thereby employing a deficit approach to diversity rather than an asset-based approach to youth and families. Because these organizations centered on the values and cultural norms of the dominant culture, they were generally led by members of the dominant culture (and many, such as Jane Addams, hailed from the elite classes of the dominant culture). Over the decades, they ended up attracting and serving youth from the majority population.

Advancing Equity in the Context of Youth Development

Legacy youth organizations face a variety of equity issues. Barriers exist that impact youth access, such as affordability, bureaucratic complexity (extensive registration paperwork, monolingual [English only] forms), or requirements for parent participation. Once youth are involved, they may face additional segregation—youth are tracked into short term programs with less sustained impact or have less access to privileges such as travel or scholarships.

These organizations often ask themselves, "How can we do more outreach to let people know about our program?" or "How do we get more of X community to participate in our programs?" It is my view that we should be asking, "What are the self-identified needs and desires of this community? and "How do we need to evolve and grow in order to partner authentically with them?" In addition, demographic change is often framed by members of dominant identities as a challenge to be tackled or as a problem to be solved. It is important to move from this deficit approach to an assets-based approach, that of seeing diversity as a strategic resource to enhance an organization's performance (Jansen, Otten, & van der Zee, 2015).

Diversity, Equality, and Equity

Equity needs to be disentangled from the closely related and often-confused concepts of diversity and equality. Diversity means the inclusion of a variety of different kinds of people in an organization. Equality is focused on ensuring that everyone gets the same resources or treatment. As Mario described it, "The person (working) at the front line has the same voice as the person at the top who's making decisions." Equity, on the other hand, addresses the root issues to ensure comparable outcomes for all: an equalizing of the balance of power, access to programs and opportunity, and allocation of resources according to people's needs. Michael provides an explanation of why we should strive for equity and not simply equality:

Equity...is different than equality. In some contexts, equality has been actually a barrier to work that needs to happen... So if we continue to... [use] the common phrase, 'Rising tides will raise all boats,' it does not work when you have started way below or you have an anchor attached to you.

If legacy organizations want to advance equity they need to do more than simply increase diversity. Youth development programs must grapple with the disparities facing marginalized youth in our society and engage in an honest assessment of how the organization may be reinforcing social inequities. They must have a willingness to make sometimes difficult changes such as re-allocating resources to where there is greater need. Even when organizations are moving in this direction, implicit biases may be at play, embedded in policies and structures. These need to be recognized and addressed to make meaningful change.

WHEN WE DO NOT EVEN KNOW WHAT WE ARE THINKING: IMPLICIT BIAS AND ITS ROLE IN EQUITY

Neurosocial research reveals that human beings are influenced constantly by both positive and negative subconscious associations about others, based on characteristics such as race, gender, age, accents, and many other aspects of identity (Staats, Capatosto, Wright, & Contractor, 2015). This phenomenon is known as implicit bias and has significant implications for our behavior and judgment. Implicit, or unconscious, biases occur involuntarily and are beyond both our awareness and our conscious control (Staats, Capatosto, Wright, & Contractor, 2015). In fact, they often are contrary to what we *think* we believe. The cause for this is that the brain has two major systems for thinking:

- System 1 is quick, instinctive, happens in the back of the brain with little effort, and tends to be highly biased because it is based on inputs from the world around us.
- System 2 thinking is slower, occurs in the front of the brain with more effort, and can serve as a brake on System 1's bias, allowing us to question our own judgments (Staats, 2015).

While everyone has implicit biases, we can address them and even mitigate their effects (Lieberman, Rock, & Cox, 2014). We need to recognize and address implicit biases, both at the organizational and individual levels. Unconscious judgments can reinforce stereotypes that either marginalize or privilege certain groups of people. Examination of these judgments helps to surface underlying beliefs which shape an organization's culture.

While it is critical that we do personal work to become aware of and challenge our own acquired judgments, it is not enough. Racism, gender bias, homophobia, sexism, ableism, and xenophobia are embedded within organizations; therefore, these need to be addressed. Even a group of highly inclusive youth workers will be stymied if they work within an organization whose policies and/or practices are at odds with the goal to create equitable and inclusive programs. Similarly, an organization may undertake major systemic changes to become more equitable, but if the staff and volunteers do not have opportunities to engage in a similar process of reflection and transformation, the process will be thwarted. For an organization to truly transform and become more inclusive and equitable, the process must include all levels of the organization.

Addressing Implicit Bias

Addressing implicit bias requires us to utilize the inherent plasticity of the brain, interrupting existing neural networks of unconscious judgments, engaging in intentional reflection, and establishing new neural networks employing "System 2" thinking using the prefrontal cortex. Josephine explains her approach:

> When I hear odd things, (I) just turn around and ask questions... I try not to argue with people about their idiosyncrasies because it's a bias that they carry, and the only way that you can deal with that is to help them to think, to bring it from the back of the head...to the front. And the only way you can do that is to ask questions. You can't get angry because we all have biases, and anger doesn't...do anything but cause people to want to hang onto their biases. So, you must engage them in thinking, you have to engage them so that they come to a different understanding.

The goal is to move people out of their System 1 thinking and engage more analytical System 2 thinking. Organizations need to provide opportunities for staff to reflect upon their initial judgments and provide a greater array of cognitive tools to help them revise their thinking.

The Power to Make Change: Organizational Disruptors

Change can come from a range of places, from leaders who have positional power within an institution or the collective power of a grassroots movement among staff and volunteers. Ultimately, change must occur at multiple levels of the organization—at the organizational/policy level and the individual staff/practitioner level.

People in a position of organizational leadership can make a powerful contribution to the work of advancing equity and addressing implicit bias by setting it as a key priority, inspiring change, and establishing accountability. Michael stated:

> I think... a systemic approach has been very successful, and I think we are starting to change the tone and the culture of the organization. I would say we took it from the top-down. At the beginning, I was the flag bearer for equity and inclusion. And it's not because there are no allies in the organization, but because I felt that it really does have to [come from] a leader. But little by little, it began to be saturated or

consumed by really wonderful folks in our organization…It is the buy-in that really makes the difference.

He makes a strong case for the role of a leader with positional power who can play the role of "organizational disrupter," who poses critical questions and interrupts the status quo in order to elicit changes. This person needs to work on multiple fronts: lead strategy, spearhead execution, and establish accountability. Teresa explains the organizational dynamics that make positional power advantageous:

> …[I]n my successful experiences working with equity, there is a level of power that has to be there in order to move the work forward. So whether it is designated staff, a leader within a department, or even a youth participant that works towards [equity], it has to be assigned…because [otherwise] it is overlooked and we are sucked into the current systems.

Equity work requires navigating systems of power so as to change them, and while this can happen from the grassroots, it is more efficient if it initially starts with a leader who has a vision and wields positional power. This is the level at which HR policies and hiring decisions can be analyzed for their impact and changed as necessary. For example, if one of the qualifications for a job is having previous experience in the organization, and if the organization lacks diversity, it is an inherent barrier to hiring more diverse staff. Simply by removing that expectation of prior work experience *within* the organization, an organization can transform its staffing.

The multiple dangers of having leaders as change agents was expressed by all interviewees: they can become the scapegoat if things do not go well; they can be overloaded and under-resourced; their colleagues can see them as the "experts" to whom everyone else then defers; or it can be seen that equity work is "their work," rather than everyone's responsibility.

Change Led by Grassroots Efforts

The reality in some organizations is that organizational change is led by the grassroots. The front-line workers closest to the community frequently are the ones with their finger on the pulse of the shifting culture, needs, and assets of the community. They also are the people who experience the dissonance that may exist between organizational policies and the needs of the community.

The challenges of this approach are that workers in large legacy organizations often do not have a platform for, or the power to, make organizational change. Grassroot change agents may face overwhelming organizational inertia based on decades of tradition. In addition, they may face significant opposition from resistant leadership, and sometimes, even more powerfully, from a vast network of alumni and volunteers who disagree with the change. Yet, when these youth workers can discover shared insights, consult directly with the community to identify needed changes, and then build collective power as a group, they are often able to advocate for meaningful changes even within a large, bureaucratic entity.

STRATEGIES FOR BUILDING
EQUITY & MITIGATING IMPLICIT BIAS

Strategies for Organizational Change

Both the interviewees for this chapter as well as the research provide recommendations for leaders who are interested in addressing implicit bias at the organizational level, and which can be used to identify and address the roots of inequities:

- *Crowdsourcing:* Groups who work together on a decision tend to make better and less biased decisions than an individual. Therefore, engaging larger numbers of people can help to reduce bias (Lieberman et al., 2014). One concrete way to do this is to expand the people involved in a hiring process in order to offer a broader array of perspectives in the process. This might include a parent, community leader, or youth participant.
- *Engaging in deliberative processing:* Implicit biases tend to be strongest in situations where a decision-maker is under time pressure or stress, so it can be helpful if the organization can intentionally slow down major decision-making processes in order to allow time for more deliberative, less biased thinking (Staats et al., 2015). One way to accomplish this in youth programs is to intentionally create a slower process for addressing disciplinary issues—having an immediate method for stopping misbehavior but having a delay before consequences are given to allow for more System 2 thinking.
- *Mitigating objectivism bias:* Known as the "blind spot bias," this is the result of believing that our experience of the world is a direct and accurate representation of how things are in the world. Because we are convinced that our version of reality is the true one, it can be extremely difficult to acknowledge other people's realities. To mitigate this type of bias, it is helpful for an organization to establish decision-making processes that intentionally engage others' perspectives by requesting outside opinions, such as a diversity officer from another organization or someone who is highly trained in diversity from a Human Resources department (Lieberman et al., 2014).
- *Mitigating self-protection bias:* Known as "in-group/out-group biases," these come from our natural tendencies to view people who are like us positively, and to have more negative perceptions of people who are different from us. These biases can be particularly harmful in organizations, especially as they diversify. One strategy for organizations to counteract this is to promote opportunities for people from different backgrounds to

highlight the values and goals that they all share. Another strategy is to have hiring processes to remove identifying features from applications to prevent potential bias (Lieberman et al., 2014).

Collective Responsibility

Josephine suggests establishing an expectation of collective responsibility as an effective strategy to ensure that everyone in an organization engages in equity. She states,.".Everyone is responsible. The leader can't make it happen until everyone in the organization is expected to drive that vision forward."

Michael describes how collective responsibility is operationalized throughout his program:

> [Working to achieve equity is] a job expectation that got included in everyone's position description, so there is nobody who doesn't have it as…part of their work. If they're not doing it, then we're going to have words…It's a big part of their review.

It is important to note that this emphasis on collective accountability was mentioned by each of my interviewees as critical for truly transforming the culture and functioning of an organization.

Colorblindness vs All-Inclusive Multiculturalism

Especially in organizations that are predominantly white, people may argue for a "colorblind" policy to promote fairness and equality among all people, regardless of background. Yet some studies have found that color-blindness can reinforce inequity (Plaut, 2014). In educational settings, for example, colorblind approaches (treating race as a taboo subject or invisible) can actually mask discriminatory classroom practices or school policies. Similarly, adults with colorblind attitudes are less likely to perceive workplace microaggressions[4] (Plaut, 2014). The fundamental flaw of a colorblind approach is that it dismisses the fact that our society and so many of its systems are not colorblind, and that people have profoundly different experiences based on their race or other aspects of their identity.

One strategy that has been shown to be effective is called all-inclusive multiculturalism. This approach includes majority members, such as people of European descent, in its definition of multiculturalism, along with people from African, Asian, Native, and Latin American descent. Rather than relegate people to being "white," it acknowledges the importance of ethnicity, and regionality, and history in the definition of "whiteness." For example, someone with a Mediterranean or

---

[4] Microaggressions are a statement, action, or incident regarded as an instance of indirect, subtle, or unintentional discrimination against members of a marginalized group such as a racial or ethnic minority.

Irish background simultaneously belongs to a distinct group with a complex and rich history, including their own experiences of oppression.

This inclusive approach appears to be more effective than traditional multiculturalism in that it can garner support from members of the majority culture (Plaut, 2014). However, the strategy is not simply about making white or other majority members feel more "comfortable," but rather about helping everyone find a common ground, understanding of and respect for their own history, and sense of belonging. Employing this approach may be particularly helpful in organizations with a high percentage of white, U.S.-born staff members.

For example, Josephine's organization has embraced a new initiative focused on engaging families who have never been involved in their programs, whether from traditionally-underserved communities or not.

> We focus more broadly than on ethnicity...it helps us to see idiosyncrasies that make it less inviting or less welcoming to young people. The approach is to recognize that there is stuff...that keeps all people from feeling like they are part of us.

This initiative has been successful in engaging staff members from rural, majority white communities, who experience many issues associated with marginalized communities such as unemployment, poverty and the opioid epidemic.

It is essential to acknowledge that changing policies and practices to make them more welcoming to the majority community will not necessarily translate to equity for marginalized communities. It should not be a way to side-step critical issues such as race and ethnicity. It cannot erase privilege or the ways that oppression is experienced by youth of color, Native American youth, immigrant youth, disabled youth, or LGBTQ youth. Addressing well-entrenched policies and practices requires assessing their impacts, and that process leads us to recognize the role of implicit bias.

For example, 4-H has built a system of competition among youth that is focused on individual performance. While this has worked well for the European-American youth who have been the majority population, there is an implicit cultural bias. The approach does not work well for youth from more collectivist cultures, including many of our immigrant communities where people value working together, rather than highlighting the efforts of only one member (Russell & Van Campen, 2011). In addition, families may not have the resources or expertise to support their child in producing a competitive project, and youth may prefer to work as part of a group where resources can be shared.

TRANSFORMATION AT THE INDIVIDUAL LEVEL

Organizations are made up of individuals and reflect their biases, as well as the sum of all the biases of those who have historically been part of the organization. In the case of legacy organizations, this can mean an accretion of over 100 years of societal and systemic racism and other prejudices. These can only be transformed by ensuring they are addressed not only at an organizational level, but also at the individual level. The following strategies were recommended by the interviewees for this chapter.

Engaging Youth

Too often, legacy organizations make the mistake of thinking that they can simply invite young people from different backgrounds into their existing programs, and then don't understand why no one comes or stays long-term. One strategy is to engage directly with the youth and community members who are the target audience, and to listen to them to get beyond biased perceptions:

> The [programs] that are not very effective, certainly, are the ones that are top-down without representation... of the youth you want to serve or the communities you want to reach. So basically, if you define a strategy, or define a program without the impacted youth...if you don't know what they need and what they want, why would [you] develop a program? (Teresa)

Through respectful and intentional community engagement, youth, their families, and other community stakeholders can have a voice and play a critical role in both identifying bias and informing change strategies. Youth and community voice are essential in mitigating the objectivism ("blind spot") biases mentioned previously, whether based on age, race, or other aspects of their identities, because they can advocate for an accurate representation of their own lived realities.

Building Relationships

One of the strongest themes that emerged from my interviews was the importance of building relationships among people from different backgrounds as a strategy to work effectively across differences. The benefits of diversity don't come from merely co-existing within the same organization, they come from having meaningful interactions that go beyond personal comfort (Bruni, 2015).

> The implicit [goal] is to get our staff in contact with [diverse] youth, so they can see that they're *youth*, so they can get past the fear.... It's amazing what happens when we have staff that sometimes have struggled with that fear, just to have contact and conversations. Their whole way of looking at the world changes. (Michael)

Teresa explains how building relationships allows individuals to participate in their own active learning, and, when relationships are established they no longer need to be mediated by someone else:

> It is more about taking time to learn from one another, intentionally... You cannot always be the cultural broker, you cannot always be the person that paves the way, because it is tiring. So how you develop opportunities for relationship building, for common understanding, will eventually eliminate bias, and your unconscious bias will certainly be diminished...

The literature offers a variety of approaches for mitigating bias at the individual level, including:

- *Intergroup contact:* Sharing experiences with people from the group about whom we have subconscious judgments and establish new associations. To be effective, the individuals should share equal status, common goals, and be in a cooperative rather than a competitive environment (Staats et al., 2015). One example of this type of experience is creating a cultural exchange between small groups of youth, volunteers, and/or staff from distinctly different backgrounds or experiences. This must be intentionally designed to equip participants with the skills to engage across difference. It also must provide meaningful opportunities for one-on-one conversations and be well-facilitated so that both areas of difference and of common ground are thoroughly explored and reflected upon. In Minnesota 4-H, this has been successful in structured dialogues between youth from rural agricultural communities and youth from urban communities.
- *Accountability:* Having the sense that one will need to justify one's decisions, feelings, or behaviors can decrease the influence of bias (Staats et al., 2015). One strategy to achieve this is implementing diverse boards and advisory committees at various levels of the organization with oversight of both programs and policies so that members of the organization know they need to explain, and perhaps advocate for, their decisions to these groups.
- *Taking perspective of others:* This strategy can reduce bias because considering others' viewpoints or considering multiple perspectives moves the brain from automatic biases into being more reflective (Staats et al., 2015). This can be practiced by either individuals or groups—engaging in a conversation about a controversial issue by first representing their own opinion, and then switching to represent the contrasting opinion of another person/group and speaking in the first person. This builds both cognitive flexibility and empathy.

When staff begin to change at the individual level, it is evident to the young participants. These strategies need to be taught and implemented, and staff and volunteers need to have opportunities to practice them on a consistent basis for them to become truly transformed.

THE IMPORTANCE OF TRAINING AND PROFESSIONAL DEVELOPMENT

As organizations strive to dispel bias and to become more diverse and equitable, training and professional development (PD) is a key strategy that connects organizational with individual change. Policy changes alone will not transform an organization. Michael expressed this interconnectedness:

...we are trying to change the culture. It's not only a system. If you go back to the research on implicit bias, it is individual, but the same processes are paralleled within a system... because systems are living organisms. So, the biases of individuals extend up to the biases of the organization. You cannot separate those. Any time you try to separate those...is when you get in trouble. That is why training has to go together with the policy change.

Training can help staff and volunteers to engage in personal reflection, confront their unconscious judgments, and transform their habits of thinking. One effective way is to develop a critical mass of individuals who are both committed to equity and connected with one another. The development of a learning cohort focused on equity and addressing implicit bias can be effective. This provides a supportive space to learn together, take risks and make mistakes, and to build an informed group of change-agents within the organization who can help address policy and practice.

Professional Learning Communities

A professional learning community (PLC) has been described in the literature as a group of practitioners who meet on a regular basis. A PLC provides an opportunity to explore critical issues in practice and to engage in "problem solving, improving practice, or learning new skills" (Vance, Salvaterra, Michelson & Newhouse, 2016). Participants of PLCs can become resources for each other, engage in inquiry about practice, and build relationships (Hill, Connolly, Akiva & McNamara, 2017). PLCs make learning more personal and concrete and helps participants grow professionally as well as gain the support they need to confront challenges (Drago-Severson et al., 2001). Within an anti-bias or pro-equity cohort, an essential focus of a PLC could be to recognize and mitigate implicit bias, both individually and collectively and to identify ways in which the organization may address biases. If the cohort engages staff at multiple levels of power within the organization and mindfully addresses the internal issues of power and privilege, it can help make new power relationships possible. In addition, a PLC can create a 'brave' space for questioning how the organization engages with power and privilege vis-a-vis youth and communities (see chapter on Critical Youth Development by Merle McGee in this book).

In my own organization, we have created two separate PLCs focused on diversity and inclusion. They have been tremendously important opportunities for staff to take risks, learn collaboratively, and create an affinity group. We have been able to engage in ongoing collaborations related to diversity and inclusion, as well as lobby for policy changes. In a study of the first annual 4-H statewide PLC (Landrieu, 2014), 100% of participants reported that they had gained a deeper understanding of their culture and privilege, were better able to understand the role of diversity and culture in their work, and had improved their ability to shift between different cultural perspectives.

Regional 4-H PLCs can have an increased focus on addressing implicit bias and addressing power and oppression. Each PLC can have a concrete impact on the larger statewide program, as well, as they take on projects such as implementing diversity and inclusion trainings for all staff at the Minnesota State Fair. PLCs demonstrate that people can make change in their own spheres of influence through individual as well as collaborative learning. They can create a collective voice to make organizational change.

CONCLUSION

To effectively serve the broad range of youth in the current population, legacy organizations must embrace equity. While it can be highly effective to have an inspirational leader spearheading change, it also can leave the organization vulnerable to relegating the work as that person's "crusade." It can be disempowering to staff and volunteers, much like adult dominance can disempower youth in youth programs. In addition, it can lessen accountability— belying the fact that members of the organization collectively have the responsibility to work on issues of equity.

On the other hand, a bottom-up approach may be more grounded in the community and led by the frontline staff who have direct contact with youth and communities, but it may not be effective at changing the higher-level policies and creating sustainable change. Ultimately, the process of organizational change will depend on leadership to provide the first impetus for change, but long-term it must be carried out at all levels of the organization if it is to be meaningful.

RESEARCH CONNECTIONS FROM THE BOOK'S EDITORS

This chapter raises some important theoretical and science-based explanations for how racism and bias can become 'hardwired' in our brains. Likewise, the chapter provides a fine-tuned analysis of the dynamics of how to change perceptions of race and privilege in legacy organizations. Kathyrn Sharpe describes both top down and bottom up approaches to program and institutional change, and the benefits and challenges of each approach.

There are multiple research questions that can be generated for advancing the investigations of organizational change to create more equity for youth, especially in legacy organizations. They include: What are the most effective strategies to engage marginalized youth and communities to provide leadership in the transformation of youth development organizations? What wisdom can we learn from organizations founded by and for marginalized communities? (Note: see chapter in this book by Jon Gilgoff). What might organizational development and change studies illuminate about the most effective processes for large organizations like these to facilitate transformation?

In this chapter, Kathryn Sharpe also points to the need for developing and offering culturally appropriate activities. For example, the U.S. is highly competitive and individualistic. Many youth programs focus on competition and awards systems for achievement and behavior. However, are these values culturally aligned with the youth that we serve, particularly immigrant youth? Kennedy et al. (2007) have written about what it takes for staff and programs to become culturally competent, e.g. the "ability to work and respond in a manner that acknowledges and respects individuals' culturally-based beliefs, attitudes, behaviors, and customs" (Kennedy et al., 2007, p.1). Some questions that arise that future research can address are "How have program activities been adapted to the cultural contexts and community values of the youth who they serve?" "How do youth practitioners come to understand and appreciate the value of the cultures of youth and families?" And, "How is cultural competency reflected in all aspects of OST programs rather than via compartmentalized events such as multicultural dinners?"

These topics will only become increasingly salient as our country undergoes demographic change and youth development organizations must find their place in it.

REFERENCES

Boy Scouts of America. (2016). *Annual report 2015*. Retrieved from http://scoutingwire.org/wp-content/uploads/2016/05/Printable%20Annual%20Report_v1.6.pdf

Bruni, F. (2015, December 12). The lie about college diversity. *The New York Times*. Retrieved from https://www.nytimes.com/2015/12/13/opinion/sunday/the-lie-about-college-diversity.html

Carr, S. (2016, June 5). Tomorrow's test: For the first time, there are more students of color than white students in our public schools. *Slate*. Retrieved from http://www.slate.com/articles/life/tomorrows_test/2016/06/american_is_becoming_a_majority_minority_nation_it_s_already_happened_in.html

Colby, S. L., & Ortman, J. M. (2015). *Projections of the size and composition of the U.S. population: 2014 to 2060*. U.S. Census Bureau. Retrieved from https://www.census.gov/content/dam/Census/library/publications/2015/demo/p25-1143.pdf

Drago-Severson, E., Helsing, D., Kegan, R., Popp, N., Broderick, M., & Portnow, K. (2001). The power of a cohort and of collaborative groups. *NCSALL Focus on Basics, 5*(B), 1–9.

Girl Scouts of America. (2017). *Annual Report 2017.* Retrieved from https://www.girlscouts.org/en/about-girl-scouts/who-we-are/facts.html

Hill, S., Connolly, J., Akiva, T., & McNamara, A. (2017). Taking it to a new level: Inquiry-based professional development as a field building enterprise. In H. J. Malone & T. Donahue (Eds.), *The growing out-of-school time field: Past, present, and future* (pp. 115–132). Charlotte, NC: Information Age Publishing.

Kennedy, E., Bronte-Tinkew, J., & Matthews, G. (2007, February). *Enhancing cultural competence in out-of-school time programs: What is it, and why is it important?* (Child Trends Research Brief No. 2007-03). Retrieved from https://www.childtrends.org/wp-content/uploads/2013/07/2007-03CulturalCompetenceOST.pdf

Jansen, W. S., Otten, S., & van der Zee, K. I. (2015). Being part of diversity: The effects of an all-inclusive multicultural diversity approach on majority members' perceived inclusion and support for organizational diversity efforts. *Group Pro-*

cesses & Intergroup Relations, 18(6), 817–832. Retrieved from https://doi.org/10.1177/1368430214566892

Landrieu, M. J. (2014). *Diversity and inclusion shared learning cohort evaluation results.* Unpublished manuscript.

Lieberman, M. D., Rock, D., Cox, C. L. (2014). Breaking bias. *NeuroLeadership Journal, 5*, 1–19. doi: 10.3389/fnhum.2012.00218 pdf.

National 4-H Council. (2017). *National 4-H Council 2016 annual report.* Retrieved from https://4-h.org/wp-content/uploads/2016/03/2016-Annual-Report.pdf

Plaut, V. C. (2014). Diversity science and institutional design. *Policy Insights from the Behavioral and Brain Sciences, 1*(1), 72–80. doi:10.1177/2372732214550164

Russell, S. T., & Van Campen, K. (2011). Diversity and inclusion in youth development: What we can learn from marginalized young people. *Journal of Youth Development, 6*(3), 96–108.

Staats, C. (2015). *Unconscious associations: Highlighting the science & real world effects of implicit bias.* Webinar for North Central Region 4-H Program Leaders.

Staats, C., Capatosto, K., Wright, R. A., & Contractor, D. (2015). *State of the science: Implicit bias review 2015.* (No. 3). Columbus, OH: Kirwan Institute for the Study of Race and Ethnicity.

Vance, F., Salvaterra, E., Michelson, J. A., & Newhouse, C. (2016, Fall). Getting the right fit: Designing a professional learning community for out-of-school time. *Afterschool Matters,* 21–32.

CHAPTER 2

ON THE LEVEL

Local Networks Creating Deeper and More Equitable School-Community Partnerships

Ken Anthony

I was a freelance reporter for a local newspaper the first time I thought about working with children and youth. I was covering a town council meeting, and someone stood up and spoke about the need for "at-risk" kids to have something to do after school. After the meeting I approached that person with an idea to create a community newspaper written by youth for youth. A few conversations later, I received a $3,000 grant to partner with the Town's Turn-On Youth Coalition and the Municipal Alliance Committee Substance Abuse Task Force to run the paper. The Turn-On Youth Coalition's role was "to advise the Mayor regarding coordination and integration of community plans and services which affect youth; provide a forum for discussion of issues related to youth; and sponsor programs to benefit youth" (Town of Piscataway, 2017, p. 7). Members of the Coalition were diverse and included representatives from the Mayor's office, municipal agencies, school districts including a teacher or school counselor and two students, businesses, citizens of the community, and mental health professionals. The Municipal Alliance Committee worked with schools and community partners to reduce alcohol and drug abuse (Town of Piscataway, 2017).

Changemakers! Practitioners Advance Equity and Access in Out-of-School Time Programs,
pages 29–44.
Copyright © 2019 by Information Age Publishing
All rights of reproduction in any form reserved.

This was in 1992, and I was 22. I had no idea what I was doing was called collaboration; the groups never talked about partnership outside a Memorandum of Understanding regarding the use of funding. The groups had a common purpose and all parties worked well together. The school counseling office and building assistant principal worked together to recruit students for the youth newspaper program, specifically targeting those with low academic averages. The town provided meeting space where youth could work on the paper, the Coalition leadership provided supplies (e.g., software, paper), and I provided volunteers to staff the paper. The school distributed a flyer about upcoming newspaper club meetings and I had monthly meetings with the Coalition, which included school staff, to discuss the project. On occasion, I presented the work of the youth newspaper program to the town council. The youth paper could be found in convenience stores, gas stations, and libraries, and the community began to notice us once we had published our second and third issues.

We didn't collect data or do any formal evaluation, but we knew that twelve to fifteen youth contributed to the paper on a regular basis. The school counselor noted increased school engagement in the students involved. Many of the students involved in the project graduated high school, which was not the direction in which they were headed when they first became involved. I saw one student a couple of years later, and he was attending Rutgers University for graphic design. Thinking about him now, I don't think it was solely his involvement with the newspaper that spurred him on to be successful. It was the joint efforts of a community that came together to offer support and guidance. This successful project demonstrates some of the essential components that we now know are important in creating effective partnerships: communication, collaboration, and leadership (Bennett, 2013; Durlak, Weissberg, & Pachan, 2010; Korobkova, 2011; Noam, Biancarosa, & Dechausay, 2003; Noam, Barry, Moellman, Dyken, Palinski, Fiore, & McCouch, 2004; Pierce, Auger, & Vandell, 2013; Vandell, Reisner, & Pierce, 2007).

While I experienced a successful collaboration, there are many more stories of failure. I believe this is due to a power imbalance between schools and community-based out-of-school time programs that impedes communication and blocks opportunities for collaboration. In order for these organizations to meaningfully connect, issues of access and equity must be acknowledged and addressed. This chapter describes the roots of and challenges inherent in this power inequity, and what can happen when these inequities begin to be balanced through meaningful power sharing and collaboration.

THE ROOTS OF POWER AND STATUS IMBALANCES

Afterschool staff employed by community-based organizations lack the credibility afforded to other school professionals (Bills, 1988). School teachers' need for legitimization in their own right and subsequent emphasis on credentialing has led to a hierarchical structure within the formal education system. When school district personnel use paraprofessionals, school teachers, in turn, enhance their own position in the organizational hierarchy, making a distinction between credentialed paraprofessionals and non-credentialed paraprofessionals (Gray & Whitty, 2010). A clear line can be drawn from the district central office starting with the Superintendent, to the building Principal, other administration, lead teachers and staff, classroom teachers, and, finally, the paraprofessional.

Most afterschool staff are viewed as paraprofessionals through the eyes of school staff. This is the case even when afterschool staff have bachelor's degrees, post-secondary degrees or other types of specialized credentials. Being viewed as paraprofessionals positions afterschool staff, by definition, lower in the school hierarchy (Bills, 1988; Gray & Whitty, 2010; Hargreaves, 1984), and inherently creates a lower status tier of the education workforce, with the afterschool professional firmly ranked on the bottom.

Due to their lower social status, district leaders and principals often fail to recognize the potential and role of afterschool programming and afterschool staff in enhancing the academic success of children and youth. They often deny staff access to resources and knowledge that would help them better support youth. They may choose not to invest in professional development for afterschool staff or give them authentic roles in the school with meaningful responsibilities. This can create a pedagogical and philosophical rift between the core school day and afterschool, which can lead to disconnected but parallel student support systems within one school building (Gray & Whitty, 2010; Vandell et al., 2007).

Out-of-school time teaching and learning environments are often categorized as complementary or alternative, but this view relegates these environments to a third or lesser space for learning (Romi & Schmida, 2009). The isolation of the classroom environment may also affect a teacher's perception of learning that takes place outside of the classroom. Hargreaves (1984) found that teachers place greater value on classroom experience compared to other environments for teaching and learning. Hargreaves theorized that teachers may view informal teaching and learning environments as culturally unacceptable, and therefore, did not consider them important. This, and other studies, demonstrate that the structure of classroom teaching in and of itself promotes teacher isolation, and relegates learning outside the classroom to a low status (Ferge, 1972; Goodlad, 1990).

Because afterschool professionals occupy the lowest rank in the education hierarchy it is more likely that school-based educators devalue afterschool staff and the environment in which they work. This makes it difficult for afterschool programs to enter partnerships with schools on equal ground; it is the root of the power and status imbalance that school-community partnerships must work against to collaborate effectively.

Mandated Partnerships

Research on the benefits of school-community collaboration has become more abundant and when collaboration occurs, it affects young people's academic and social gains (Bennett, 2015; Vandell, Reisner & Pierce, 2007).

As a result, funders are increasingly making partnerships between schools and community-based organizations a requirement at the local, state, and national level (American Savings Foundation, 2017; Connecticut State Department of Education, 2017a).

The federally funded 21st Century Community Learning Centers (21CCLC) provide services to youth attending high-poverty, low-performing schools including academic enrichment activities that can help students meet state and local achievement standards, drug and violence prevention programs, career and technical programs, counseling, art, music, and recreation programs, STEM programs, and character education (Afterschool Alliance, 2017). The 21st CCLC Request for Proposals (RFP) requires links between schools and community-based organizations. In one model the community-based organization (CBO) runs the afterschool program at the school. In the other, and most prevalent model, schools or districts receive 21st CCLC dollars to run the program and then subcontracts with community partners.

Some state funding also mandates collaboration between schools and afterschool programs. One such example is the state of Connecticut. The state provides afterschool grants, and the request for proposal (RFP) requires school-community partnerships (Connecticut State Department of Education, 2017b). While the depth of partnership varies from community to community, these efforts are realized through a system of local philanthropic, school district, and state funding streams. Private foundations at times require grantees to collaborate to receive funding. The American Savings Foundation, for example, in New Britain, Connecticut makes school-community partnerships a centerpiece of their funded programs.

Given the research highlighting the benefits of collaboration, it is understandable why funders want to encourage partnerships between schools and community-based organizations. However, even when funders require collaboration implementation is problematic and power inequities remain.

Building School-Community Relationships

According to Noam, Biancarosa, and Dechausey (2003), there is a continuum of school-community partnerships. Their "Bridging Intensity Typology" measures alignment of school and afterschool programs. At one end of the spectrum are self-contained community-based afterschool programs, that make little attempt to collaborate with schools (and *vice versa*). Other points on the spectrum include associated, coordinated, integrated, and finally unified programs (Noam et al., 2003). Noam and colleagues assert that if there is a "systemic or institutional" relationship between the program and the school where each has, "identified each other as an important partner in achieving their goals around learning and other aspects of development" the program is considered integrated (Noam, et al.,2003, p. 26). The last tier, unified programs, represent a seamless learning day, with little differentiation between the school and afterschool environment (Noam et al., 2003).

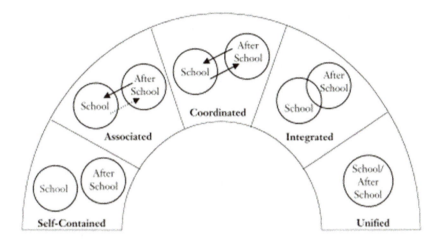

FIGURE 2.1.   For Noam, the unified program represents a successful school-community partnership. (reprinted with permission)

We are just beginning to understand how to reach the unified stage. Bennett's (2015) research identifies key aspects of alignment. The study collected data from 75 sites in 11 districts from over 8,000 students to measure alignment between school and afterschool programs. She found that when principals and afterschool site coordinators had a shared sense of partnership, communication structures, and shared academic resources, children performed better on standardized tests. A strong partnership, as identified in this study, includes deep, regular communication about students going beyond the typical interactions about attendance and behavior. It also includes sharing academic resources such as websites, curriculum, and teaching strategies between the school and afterschool staff. Misalignment of these factors had a correlational impact on students' academic success, as students at those sites showed lower test performance.

According to Bennett, "strongly aligned" programs are more integrated than unified, as per Noam and colleagues' typology. She also goes on to state that "alignment does not equal unification, because afterschool programs are not an extension of the school day, but rather a unique learning space that is deeply aligned to the culture and learning of the school day" (T. Carmichael [formally Bennett], personal communication, January 2, 2018).

Additional research on this topic (Anthony & Morra, 2016) identified several barriers that impede successful school-afterschool partnerships. These include a lack of time delegated to meetings and interactions, lack of formal communication structures, and misconceptions about one another. Strategies to enhance partnerships included the existence of communication structures, afterschool staff having access to school teams on the part of afterschool staff, access to student planning and assessment, and collaborative funding opportunities. Formal check-in meetings and data sharing agreements are also some examples of effective partnership strategies. Creating a deeper sense of partnership and establishing ongoing communication enables afterschool programs to have a seat at the table as an equal and contributing partner with school administration, staff, and teachers.

The Role of School Leadership

By and large, school climate and culture are largely dictated by school principals. Newmann, Kings, and Young (2000) created a five-component leadership framework based on observations and interviews with school leaders and staff in nine low-income, low-achieving elementary schools. The framework puts principals squarely in the center; they are the ones who connect teachers with opportunities to build knowledge, skills, and dispositions. They have access to professional development emphasizing capacity building, technical resources that help to build a professional community, and program coherence. The principal is responsible for creating community partnerships to connect learning to the world outside of the school and make learning more relevant. However, with the increased emphasis on test scores, principals often do not have the needed hours to implement systemic change or create meaningful relationships with other community organizations.

Samuelson (2007) describes the roles of principals in creating and maintaining school-afterschool connections. These include facilitating regular communication, serving as liaison between school and afterschool staff, and presenting the afterschool program as an integral part of the school. The key takeaways from this study are the importance of an effective afterschool coordinator, and the critical nature of the principal-coordinator relationship. For an effective relationship, principals must be willing to cede power to the afterschool coordinator to ensure a smooth transition between the school day and afterschool hours. The afterschool site coordinator, working in conjunction with the principal, needs to align behavioral expectations between the two realms and generate consistent messages to reinforce a sense of partnership. This takes an afterschool coordinator who is able to take the lead in scheduling meetings with school leadership and actively advocating the importance of afterschool to support common goals. Additionally, the site coordinator must be able to lead their staff and clarify roles and work as a team to evaluate the needs of children and families. The relationship, however, between coordinator and principal, to be effective, must be bidirectional, requiring a commitment from both school and afterschool leadership.

Power Disparities on the Ground

In my nine years as technical assistance provider and convener for the Connecticut After School Network, I frequently hear about the lack of partnership between afterschool providers and schools. My observation is that this lack largely depends on the amount of intentional bridging between the school and afterschool staff. Several factors impede the development of meaningful partnerships, including school hierarchy, funding differences, little to no sense of partnership, and a lack of understanding regarding the implementation of classroom and afterschool program practices (Anthony & Morra, 2016).

The imbalance of power between school and afterschool programs manifests itself in several ways. This includes vying over shared space (room use/turf issues), lack of time (for meetings/planning between school personnel and afterschool staff), and the lack of recognition of expertise on the part of school personnel towards afterschool staff. The positioning and relationship between these two entities impacts how the goals, beliefs, and pedagogy of the afterschool program are shared or aligned with school goals and youth outcomes. A lack of communication and coordination has the effect of widening the power imbalances between the school and afterschool arenas.

To correct the imbalance, school and afterschool professionals need to see the day as a learning continuum rather than designated blocks of time for learning (the school day) supplemented by other activities that do not include learning (after school). Trust must be built by creating opportunities for collaborative learning and communication between school and afterschool personnel (Samuelson, 2007). In addition, afterschool staff must be involved in the school community, and both sides need opportunities to share knowledge and practice. Finding the time to do this takes work and is potentially the largest obstacle (Anthony & Morra, 2016).

Increasingly, communities are looking for ways to impact children and families more systematically and holistically. The child and his/her developmental needs are the same whether in school during the day, attending an afterschool program, summer camp, or community health center. Local intermediary networks, like the Coalition for New Britain's Youth, is one model that can intentionally connect all of these spheres.

A LOCAL INTERMEDIARY NETWORK: COALITION FOR NEW BRITAIN'S YOUTH

The Local Context

New Britain, Connecticut is a small city of approximately 73,000 people. It has a racially diverse population, comprised of 48% White non-Hispanic, 37% Hispanic, and 13% Black (U.S. Census Bureau, 2016). According to the 2012 U.S. Census, 20% of the residents are foreign born and 50% reported a language other than English spoken at home. Economically, New Britain is a post-industrial small urban center similar to many other cities in the Northeast. The per capita income was reported to be $20,601 in 2012 dollars (U.S. Census Bureau, 2016), compared to the state level of $37,627. Twenty-three percent of its residents live

TABLE 2.1.

Race/ethnicity	64% Hispanic
	18% Caucasian
	14% Black or African American.
English language learners	16%
Homes where English is not primary language	50%
Living below poverty level	78%
Quality for free or reduced price meals	71%

below the poverty level, which is more than double the state poverty level of 10% (U.S. Census Bureau, 2016).

There are 14 schools within the Consolidated School District of New Britain (CSDE), with 10,071 students (Connecticut State Department of Education, 2017c). Table 2.1 reveals the school demographics. While the graduation rate has been steadily rising to 64% in 2014, this was still considerably lower than the state average of 88%.

The Coalition for New Britain's Youth

The Coalition for New Britain's Youth (The Coalition) is a city network that was intentionally formed in 2006 to bring all providers together to serve youth. The initial collaboration was facilitated by The American Savings Foundation, in response to a request from multiple community-based youth agencies. According to Maria Sanchez of the American Savings Foundation, there was an "overarching need to talk with other [afterschool] providers… they wanted the Foundation to organize them two times per year for common professional development through an Afterschool Academy" (Maria Sanchez, personal communication, August 31, 2017). Over the past twelve years the Coalition helped to create and streamline processes for afterschool providers such as shared student recruitment and retention strategies. As time passed, the Coalition brought in partners from other sectors including the Community Mental Health Affiliates (CMHA), Parent Leadership for Educational Achievement (PLEA), and other community agencies.

The Early Years

In the early years of partnership, the primary goal was to avoid duplication of services to best utilize funding. Everyone agreed this was a priority, but when it came to sharing resources, it was a challenge. Several agencies had never partnered together, in fact they had competed with each other for funding. Programs struggled to enroll youth who needed services, and the schools did not feel it was their role to recruit students to participate in afterschool programs. Agencies had not adequately articulated the importance of the work, and the district did not see the value and potential of the relationship. The status inequity between schools and afterschool programs was at the forefront, and as one Coalition founder shared, "the message to community partners was initially 'we are the education experts and we are responsible for outcomes, you take care of after school.'"

Righting the Power Imbalance

The power imbalances began to shift with the advent of the Summer Enrichment Experience (SEE) and the creation of a school district office for community partnerships. The Summer Enrichment Experience (SEE) program, spearheaded by the district superintendent, helped struggling children in the district and provided additional support for families. It involved all partners of the Coalition. SEE's outcomes included a decrease in student chronic absenteeism and increase in students' reading proficiency. Because of this success, the school district became more invested as a member of the Coalition. Under the leadership of the superintendent, school-community partnerships became an intentional strategy to help close the opportunity gap within New Britain. It led to the creation of joint activities to equalize the power dynamic and sustain the school-community partnership.

Joint Activities

Joint professional development is a key strategy to unify an organization's vision. The Coalition hosted joint professional development sessions for all members. It has begun to look at common achievement measures and shared curriculum. As partnerships have deepened, the Coalition members have come together to collectively apply for funding. For example, the Coalition has partnered with other community providers such as CMHA to examine the role trauma and equity play in student success and has secured funding through the Fund for Greater Hartford (Werth, 2017). The Consolidated School District of Britain partnered with the Coalition when they took part in a study examining school-afterschool alignment (Anthony & Morra, 2016). After the results were shared with the community, the school district and Coalition reviewed recommendations and created an action plan modeled intentionally on the components of the Bennett (2015) framework.

As a result of the Coalition's work, New Britain was recognized twice as an All American City by the National Civic League, is now a Campaign for Grade Level Reading Pacesetter Community, and received an award from the National Summer Learning Association for its SEE program.

What It Took to Create & Sustain Partnerships

In preparing for this chapter, I spoke with school, community, and local philanthropic leaders in New Britain who have been involved with the Coalition. We discussed lessons learned and strategies for success. In the analysis of these conversations, six distinct areas emerged that can provide guidelines for developing and sustaining partnerships.

1. Create a System for Accountability and Data Collection

The American Savings Foundation investment of over $1 million in 2006 to support afterschool initiatives in New Britain built accountability and data collection into their RFP. In an effort to leverage the partnership between the school and community provider, the Foundation developed joint data sharing agreements and memoranda of understanding (MOU) that spelled out outcome measurements and other requirements (M. Sanchez, personal communication, August 31, 2017). The MOU provided clarity for the partnership and laid out district and CBO expectations. One MOU required the use of a common tool for program assessment. A system was created between the school, community leadership, and staff whereby the district information technology department created an afterschool dashboard as part of the district data systems. These data have been used to target the lowest 20th percentile of students for the district summer program and assist in student recruitment for the afterschool programs. In another example, joint professional development for behavior and classroom management strategies, were offered to school and afterschool staff, and afterschool staff were welcomed into meetings regarding student attendance issues at the school.

2. Create a Mutual Language and Overcome Perceptual Barriers

Initially there were "language and perceptual barriers" between the schools and afterschool program staff (Maria Sanchez, personal communication, 2017). Even though the goals of school and afterschool staff were similar, differing terminology made it a struggle to communicate. According to Kim Russo, Executive Director of the Fund for Greater Hartford, the Coalition played the role of "translator when convening the school and community partners" (K. Russo, personal communication, August 31, 2017).

As the agencies continued their collaboration, some of the language barriers were addressed, and they developed a shared language. Each school year and prior to summer programming, CBO partners contacted District Curriculum Intervention teachers. This conversation helped to align the afterschool activities with the school day curriculum and align skills taught during the afterschool program with State Standards for learning. Though the district is unable to share individual student data, it sends community partners the names and addresses of students who could benefit from afterschool programs. These are the first students invited to participate in activities. Perceptually, the district now views the afterschool programs differently, "as an important component for a child's safety" and "as [educational] interventions for students" (N. Puglisi, personal communication, September 7, 2017).

3. Create Structures for Resource Sharing

The Coalition has established structures for resource sharing. For example, the Youth and Workforce Strategy Group has developed a partnership with the district that allows school administrative staff to attend Coalition meetings and make decisions in place of having duplicative meetings to discuss next steps (P. Fox, personal communication, September 5, 2017). In addition, community-based organizations, such as the Opportunities Industrialization Center (OIC) of New Britain now offer credit-bearing afterschool programs for high school students. This has required ongoing negotiations and structured conversations between CBOs, high schools, and district administration.

4.   Develop Clear Roles and Responsibilities

Clear roles for the partnership help make it run smoothly. Maggie Winiarski, Afterschool Program Coordinator for New Britain Parks and Recreation, which has an afterschool program in all elementary and middle schools in the district, mentioned that Coalition works to "align all afterschool programs with a clear vision and mission that identifies roles and responsibilities of each agency in the coordination of afterschool programming" (M. Winiarski, personal communication, September 7, 2017). Some of the joint responsibilities include recruiting and hiring staff, identifying and recommending students, curricular alignment with the school through working with the District Curriculum Coordinator, setting bi-monthly progress meetings between the school administration and parks and recreation staff, attending professional development offered by the Coalition, and creating attendance reports that are accessed by the district and CBOs.

5.   Create a True Partnership

True partnership does not happen overnight; it takes continual work and community engagement. According to Nancy Sarra, Superintendent at the Consolidated School District of New Britain, "You have to be actively engaged in the community, it starts with meeting two or three people…it starts with a lot of talking and ongoing communication. What started as coffee (together) has turned into monthly breakfast meetings. (We have) a shared vision. One of the key questions we ask is what will be the successful New Britain High School graduate…how do we define those attributes, and how do we merge Coalition and District plans?" (N. Sarra, personal communication, September 5, 2017).

Over the past several years outreach to and input from the community has become more of a priority for the District. According to Tracey Madden-Hennesey, Associate Director of the YWCA of New Britain, "there is a prioritizing of community voice in planning what is needed in the school district" (Madden-Hennesey, personal communication, August 29, 2017). This has led to multiple opportunities, such as community providers and members of the Coalition being invited to a district convocation and being recognized in front of all district staff. A major impact of the partnership is that the district instituted a Community Partnership Department to create better linkages between schools and community.

6. Cultivate formal and informal leaders

The role of leadership in the Coalition is critical. The American Savings Foundation, which originally convened the afterschool providers, provided the first leadership. The original network members included senior leadership from the New Britain YWCA, United Way, American Savings Foundation, the superintendent and assistant superintendent of the school district, among others. These individuals took on the responsibility for creating dialogue as well as assumed leadership roles, serving as chair, vice-chair, treasurer, and secretary respectively.

Paulette Fox, Executive Director of OIC, discussed the importance of, "identifying the formal leaders who can make change and the informal leaders who can leverage change…informal leaders can push for change and have the trust of stakeholders in the community" (P. Fox, personal communication, August 31, 2017). When the school district first got involved, they played a limited role in developing the network. Fortuitously, the superintendent of schools was promoted from building principal to director of curriculum and instruction, and then to superintendent. She was able to use her knowledge of the community landscape to shape a role for the district within afterschool systems efforts. Having worked with many of the community providers during her tenure as principal, she had the trust of key stakeholders and used her leadership position to align efforts between the school district and community based organizations.

BARRIERS AND CHALLENGES TO PARTNERSHIP

The chief barriers to school-afterschool cooperation within the Coalition were school personnel's perceptions of the qualifications of the afterschool staff and difficulty sharing space with afterschool programs. Eliminating these barriers falls squarely on both the school and afterschool staff. Having an effective site coordinator and developing a shared vision with school personnel is critical in creating partnership. While the Coalition has worked to reduce the assumption of differences of practice and knowledge through joint professional development and involves the district in planning efforts, these site level barriers remain. As mentioned earlier, the hierarchical nature of the formal education system perpetuates these issue and the subsequent inequities.

The afterschool system itself can reify and perpetuate these perceptions. There is a chronic lack of consistency in both the quality and retention of afterschool staff. According to Huang and Cho (2010), having qualified, motivated staff is a key indicator of quality. However, finding and keeping effective site-coordinators (as well as direct service staff) is not easy with the part time hours and low pay typically seen across programs. In order to create equitable partnerships between school and afterschool staff, these perceptions and structural barriers must be overcome. One way New Britain has addressed this perception is to bring together certified teachers and community based professionals to work collaboratively on projects, such as the Summer SEE program. Another strategy to mitigate the power imbalance is co-teaching. For example, the newly created Extreme Summer Program that targets middle school students adopted a co-teaching model where school and afterschool professionals work side-by-side. These collaborative programs are still, however, quite rare.

CONCLUSION

The Coalition has evolved through the years to develop relationships built on a common vision. While some barriers still exist, and collaboration may at times be challenging, the Coalition is an example of how a local city network can help promote and institutionalize change within a community. These efforts take research, collaboration, and systems thinking. As a practitioner, I have seen the impact that collaboration and coordination can have on afterschool programming. The reality is that school-community partnerships take work, need to be intentional, and are rarely perfect.

Creating equitable partnerships involve collaboration at all levels (state/local/ district/CBO) and investment in a larger vision. Afterschool professionals need to be recognized for their contribution to the holistic development of children. Afterschool site coordinators and staff need to be intentional about the connections they are making with the school beyond attendance and behavioral referrals. They must become part of the community fabric, and make sure that they communicate well, and often, about the assets and resources they bring to the school to help achieve school goals.

Local networks, like the Coalition, can help to create a more equitable space to examine practice, ask questions, implement activities with fidelity, assess and re-evaluate and tweak program design. Structures created by networks such as joint professional development and cross-sector committees can help mitigate the imbalance of power between schools and CBOs and create a partnership focused on possible solutions and strategies. A network can facilitate substantive conversations beyond attendance and behavioral issues such as discussions of quality and continuous improvement. Networks can also create more formalized systems such as regular meetings, joint professional development, and collaborative program planning and implementation.

This chapter about the New Britain Coalition may provide insight and hope for other communities. The story illustrates what collaboration and systems building can look like on the ground and can be a practical resource for practitioners wanting to increase equity in their own school-community partnerships.

RESEARCH CONNECTIONS FROM THE EDITORS

Little attention has been paid to city-wide networks, like the Coalition, that promote the overall well-being of youth. One exception is that of the Wallace Foundation which funded five cities: Boston, Chicago, New York City, Providence, and Washington, D.C. The goals of the initiative were to "increase access to and participation in OST programs; improve the quality of OST programs; build an information, technology, and communication infrastructure to facilitate better management and support for OST programs; and work toward sustaining OST programs and the systems designed to support them" (McCombs et al., 2010, p. iii). However, it's important to note that these networks are primarily within the OST context, and focus primarily at the system level such as data sharing across organizations. The Wallace funded cities didn't extend to other fields to provide a comprehensive approach to working with youth, such as the inclusion of health organizations and other large social service agencies, e.g. those of court-involved youth/juvenile justice.

What makes this chapter unique is the focus on (in)equity between organizations, and how this needs to be recognized and addressed in order for the network to succeed. The relationship between schools and afterschool programs has always been talked about among practitioners as being highly problematic, mostly via anecdotes (Dilles, 2010). Yet it's rarely been studied or written about with a scholarly and intentional focus. This chapter's examination of the roots of these problematic relationships and power struggles is therefore a valuable contribution to the literature, and can be a springboard for much more research.

Research questions abound. For example, what power dynamics emerge in extended day schools that create and sustain inequities between school day personnel and afterschool personnel? How do these power dynamics ultimately affect the quality of programs and the services for youth? Would introducing certification of afterschool program staff, or credit-bearing degrees continue to relegate them to that of a lower status in the eyes of school day teachers? Will breaking down silos—education, health, juvenile justice—in networks such as described in this chapter affect youth outcomes? We need to investigate and write more about these community and municipal networks that promote community as well as youth well-being.

REFERENCES

Afterschool Alliance. (2017). *21st century community learning centers: Providing local afterschool and summer programs for families.* Retrieved from http://www.afterschoolalliance.org/policy21stcclc.cfm

American Savings Foundation. (2017). *After school program grants.* Retrieved from http://www.asfdn.org/after-school-grants-howto.php.

Anthony, K., & Morra, J. (2016). Creating holistic partnerships between school and afterschool. *Afterschool Matters, 24*(1), 33–42.

Bennett, T. L. (2013). *Examining levels of alignment between school and afterschool and associations on student academic achievement* (Unpublished doctoral dissertation). Irvine, CA: University of California, Irvine.

Bennett, T L. (2015). Examining levels of alignment between school and afterschool and associations on student academic achievement. *Journal of Expanded Learning Opportunities, 1*(2), 4–22.

Bills, D. (1988). Credentials and capacities: Employers perceptions of the acquisition of skills. *The Sociological Quarterly, 29*(3), 439–449. https://doi.
org/10.1111/j.1533-8525.1988.tb01263.x

Connecticut State Department of Education. (2017a). *21ˢᵗ century community learning centers grant program request for proposals.* Retrieved from http://www.sde.ct.gov/
sde/lib/sde/pdf/rfp/rfp132_21st_cclc_2016.pdf

Connecticut State Department of Education. (2017b). *After school grant program request
for proposals.* Retrieved from http://www.sde.ct.gov/sde/lib/sde/pdf/rfp/rfp999_af-
ter_school_grant_program_2017.pdf.

Connecticut State Department of Education. (2017c). *District profile and performance
report 2016–17, New Britain school district.* Retrieved from http://edsight.ct.gov/
Output/District/HighSchool/0890011_201516.pdf/

Dilles, L. S. (2010, Fall). Can we talk? Creating effective partnerships between school and
afterschool programs. *Afterschool Matters, 12,* 51–54.

Durlak, J. A., Weissberg, R. P., & Pachan, M. (2010). A meta-analysis of afterschool programs that seek to promote personal and social skills in children and adolescents.
American Journal of Community Psychology, 45, 294–309. doi: 10.1007/s10464-
010-9300-6

Ferge, S. (1972). How teachers perceive the relation between school and society. *Sociology
of Education, 45*(1), 1–22. doi: 10.307/2111829

Goodlad, J. (1990). Better teachers for our nation's schools. *The Phi Delta Kappan, 72*(3),
184–194.

Gray, S., & Whitty, G. (2010). Social trajectories or disrupted identities? Changing and
competing models of teacher professionalism under new labour. *Cambridge Journal
of Education, 40*(1), 5–23. doi:10.1080/03057640903567005

Hargreaves, A. (1984). Experience counts, theory doesn't: How teachers talk about their
work. *Sociology of Education, 57*(4), 244–254. DOI: 10.2307/2112428

Huang, D., & Cho, J. (2010). Using professional development to enhance staff retention.
Afterschool Matters, 12(2), 9–16.

Korobkova, K. (2011, Fall) Getting in alignment. *AfterSchool Today, 2*(3), 14–15.

McCombs,J. S., Bodilly, S. J., Orr, N.,Scherer, E., Constant, L., & Gershwin, D. (2010).
Profiles of five cities improving after-school programs through a systems approach.
Hours of Opportunity, *Vol. 3.* Santa Monica, CA: The Rand Corporation.

Newmann, F., King, B., & Youngs, P. (2000). Professional development that addresses
school capacity: Lessons from urban elementary schools. *American Journal of Education, 108*(4), 259–99.

Noam, G., Biancarosa, G., & Dechausay, N. (2003). *Afterschool education: Approaches to
an emerging field.* Cambridge, MA: Harvard Education Press.

Noam, G., with Barry, S., Moellman, L.W., Dyken, L., Palinski, C., Fiore, N., & McCouch,
R. (2004, Spring). The Four Cs of Afterschool Programming A New Case Method
for a New Field. *Afterschool Matters, 2*(Spring), 1–19.

Pierce, K., Auger, A., & Vandell, D. (2013). *Associations between structured activity participation and academic outcomes in middle childhood: Narrowing the achievement
gap?* Irvine, CA: University of California, Irvine.

Romi, S., & Schmida, M. (2009). Non-formal education: A major educational force in
the postmodern era. *Cambridge Journal of Education, 39*(2), 257–273. doi/
abs/10.1080/03057640902904472

Samuelson, L. (2007, Spring). After the last bell: The role of principals in school-based afterschool programs. *Afterschool Matters, 6*, 6–14.

Town of Piscataway. (2017). *Citizen leadership form.* Retrieved from: http://www.piscat-awaynj.org/sites/piscatawaynj.org/files/pway_files/global/documents/Citizen Leadership Form REV 09112012.pdf

U.S. Census Bureau. (2016). *New Britain, Connecticut quickfacts.* Retrieved from: http://www.census.gov/quickfacts/table/PST045215/0950370.

Vandell, D., Reisner, E., & Pierce, K. (2007). *Outcomes linked to high-quality afterschool programs: Longitudinal findings from the study of promising afterschool programs.* Washington, DC: Policy Studies Associates. Retrieved from http://www.eric.ed.gov/PDFS/ED499113.pdf.

Werth, J. (2017). To be a trauma-informed city takes a cultural shift and partnership. *The CT Mirror.* Retrieved from: https://ctmirror.org/2017/08/28/to-be-a-trauma-in-formed-city-takes-a-cultural-shift-and-partnership/

CHAPTER 3

EXTENDING A MIGHTY HAND

Outreach and Retention Strategies to Help Our Least Supported Youth

Rachel Loeper

I met Sharlene while assembling furniture a week before Mighty Writers opened its doors in 2009. An eight-year-old with a tight ponytail, sweaty from playing at the park around the corner, she walked right through our front door.

"What is this place?" she demanded.

Behind Sharlene trailed four younger children from the neighborhood: her sister, a cousin, and a couple of other friends. Sharlene was clearly in charge.

"It's a writing center," I said, smiling. "We're going to write poetry and comic books and music lyrics. We open next week!"

Sharlene looked around suspiciously, eyeing the new furniture, stocked shelves and comic book rack.

"Who's it for?" she asked, with the air of a reporter asking a "gotcha question."

Mighty Writers (MW) was, of course, for her and her friends, kids who were wandering the neighborhood with a confident 8-year-old in charge, kids who, in the middle of summer, didn't appear to be enrolled in summer camp or have regular supervision.

Changemakers! Practitioners Advance Equity and Access in Out-of-School Time Programs,
pages 45–58.
Copyright © 2019 by Information Age Publishing
45

Sharlene sat with me for about 15 minutes that day, and each child left with a book or comic and some program information. They came back the next day, and I let them in. We were open after all, despite my best laid plans.

It took another year or two for Sharlene to feel at home at MW, but eventually, she trusted that we weren't going to disappear. Years later, as a teen, she wrote:

> I've been going to Mighty Writers for six years and together we make a big family. They made me feel welcome. Mighty Writers brought me so much joy. They were a pair of helping hands with my writing. They helped me get higher points on my essays. I wrote poems at home that I shared with Mighty Writers. They really enjoyed my poem called "Lost."

OUTREACH AND RETENTION IN OUT-OF-SCHOOL TIME

Multiple factors influence why youth, especially older youth, choose to participate or not participate in out-of-school time (OST) programs. A review of the research reveals few surprises. Older youth participate because of positive relationships with staff and other youth, high-quality programming, and fun (Borden et al., 2005; Deschenes et al., 2010; Hall et al., 2015; Pearson, Russell, & Reisner, 2007, Sanzone et al., 2011; White House Council for Community Solutions 2012). Youth are prevented from participating due to school, family, and work obligations (all of which grow in correlation with the family's level of poverty), financial need, and transportation issues (Borden et al. 2005, 2006; International Youth Foundation, 2016; Perkins et al., 2007).

A study by Lewis and Burd-Sharps (2015) on youth disconnection from opportunity summarized key challenges to youth participation. They write, "Place matters. Race matters. But…the combination of the two really packs a wallop" (p. 16). That is, concentrated racial segregation has dramatic but very different consequences for young people. And this difference is based in part on the distance to opportunity—not only physical distance but also social and aspirational distance.

Youth practitioners must mitigate and navigate each of these distances to increase youth participation in OST programs and create greater equity: physical distance, social distance, and aspirational distance. Physical distance is real; and simply providing transportation helps. Social distance is pervasive; youth who have never visited a college don't usually dream of attending one. Aspirational distance, I believe, is overblown: most parents want what is best for their children and understand that education is one key to success. Our job as youth organizations is to tap into and build upon these aspirational needs of young people.

Too much research on program participation among ethnic minority youth falls victim to the tired narrative that youth programs "keep kids off the streets" or help them "stay out of trouble." Sometimes, these words come right from the mouths of young people (Borden et. al 2005, 2006; Perkins et al., 2007). I've heard these words myself, but I've always had the impression I was being fed a line youth thought I wanted to hear. It's a narrative that they may hear at home and certainly in popular culture. It's a hollow trope, and not one that comes up when engaged in a personal and meaningful dialogue with a young person.

While quality OST programs certainly must keep kids safe at minimum, I question tolerating programs that are merely safe places. Our kids deserve more. At Mighty Writers, we create safe spaces with positive relationships, high-quality programming, and fun. Despite this, we have struggled with outreach and retention, particularly for youth who need the most help. This chapter will explore the challenges of outreach and retention and analyze the roots of the challenges. I propose that poor outreach and retention are the foundations of inequity—if youth can't access high quality services, we are perpetuating social and academic achievement gaps rather than helping to close them. Finally, the chapter will provide some suggestions and recommendations for tried and true ways that have emerged in my organization over the past nine years. It is the hope that these recommendations can be adapted by other programs to reach high-need youth.

THE HISTORY OF MIGHTY WRITERS

During the winter of 2008–09, I organized a series of morning coffee dates and evening happy hours for writers and teachers in Philadelphia. I knew about Philadelphia's literacy crisis (at the time only 24% of 4th and 8th graders were reading and writing proficiently). I thought a community writing center was the answer. Into one of these happy hours walked a Mighty Writers board member. "I know a guy named Tim Whitaker," he said. "He's looking to do something similar and he has the money to do it."

I had about 100 volunteers, a gaggle of kids from the school where I taught. I also had the offer of a storefront in a historically African American neighborhood. Tim had recently left journalism (he had been the editor of Philadelphia Weekly for a decade). He had taken the much more logical approach to starting a nonprofit: finding the seed money first. Our assets and vision were a natural fit.

Did I want to get paid for something I was willing to do for free? I didn't hesitate. We met in April, 2009, and swung open our doors that summer. Twelve youth writing workshops were booked to capacity in our storefront that first summer.

As MW programs developed, we began to attract professional writers as volunteers to work with participants. As a result, more well-supported youth began to come through our doors. These included kids from the local charter school who stopped by for college essay night, fourth graders gearing up to apply to prestigious magnet schools, and sixth graders writing novellas. The newer participants were from stable, middle-class families who were able to find MW easily because their parents had time to proactively seek resources. It didn't mean they needed us any less; many of them struggled and benefitted from the MW community. But it raised the question: how would we as an organization ensure that we continued to serve Philadelphia's high-need youth, even as our neighborhoods gentrified, and our volunteers became recognizable authors?

Back to Sharlene. Compared to other, more well-supported students, Sharlene struggled. She was held back in second grade. Her dad's need for dialysis put a strain on a family already strapped financially. They had all of the additional trauma and burdens that come with poverty: too many people in the house, too little food and attention. Sharlene struggled, but she also showed up every day. She was integral to our community. She was a discerning critic but also eager to help make things better. She was a quick friend to anyone who didn't have one and a tentative poet who found her first true writing confidence in short, thoughtful poetic lines. Sharlene is the kind of high-need participant that we wanted to reach and keep in our programs. We know we can have an impact on kids with the odds stacked against them. Indeed, this is the original core mission of MW, and the one that drives, and should be driving, our programming.

High-quality, relevant programming misses the mark if it only serves students who are already supported and engaged. An outreach and retention plan that reaches out to, and creates access for, our least supported youth is vital to our mission. In every neighborhood there are kids like Sharlene. It is the responsibility of program staff to find them in the streets and local schools. Staff reluctant to develop and implement a strong outreach plan reflects an unwillingness to do the most difficult and yet rewarding kind of OST work. Much worse, the reluctance creates, and perpetuates, inequity in access and resources.

OUTREACH CHALLENGES

There are multiple challenges in recruiting and retaining youth living in poverty who may lack access to educational opportunities. The following have been our biggest challenges.

Enrollment

MW has struggled to get families[1] who are eligible and in need of our services to enroll their children. The reasons for this are many: they don't know about the program, they don't see the value, or getting their children physically to the program is beyond their capability or income. We also have families who register their children but don't show up for the program. There was a mother who, several years ago, signed her two children up for every program we offered. After a year of phone calls and inquiries and no response, I stopped adding them to the class lists, but their sign-ups kept rolling in. We had the mom's email and continued to share opportunities whenever they arose.

When I finally met her, more than two years after she began submitting enrollment forms, I exclaimed that I felt like I was meeting a celebrity. She'd finally made it in! I met her kids and welcomed them like celebrities, as well. Later, she

---

[1] Families in this context include a range of configurations, including single head of households, grandparents raising grandchildren, etc.

shared that she was overwhelmed by single motherhood and always signed her kids up late at night, after they were in bed, for programs to which she hoped she would have the strength to bring them by the time the program started. But she inevitably was overwhelmed by a sick child or struggling family member, or couldn't afford the public transportation to get to our site, or could barely muster the strength to get dinner on the table that night. But she persisted, and so did we.

Understanding the Mission

A hurdle to successful outreach is staff understanding, and often misunderstanding, the agency's mission and role. New staff and volunteers often come to us expecting that all of our young people will be fully engaged in activities and self-identify as writers. Not so. We have students with learning disabilities, behavior problems, and students who are several grade levels behind in reading and writing. We do have some star writers, but many of them have grown into that through years of participating in MW's programs and working hard on their writing. We often hear the question, from new staff members and volunteers alike, "Do the kids want to be here?" The answer is simple: it is our job, as staff members and volunteers, to create the relationships, environment, and programs that make them want to come back.

Staff Backgrounds

I am reluctant to hire staff members who come from different socioeconomic, cultural, religious or ethnic backgrounds than our youth. Staff who don't share common reference points with the families are quicker to blame parents (and communities) when children don't attend, or dole out severe consequences for youth behaviors. They are also quicker to engage in power struggles with kids, parents, and even our volunteers.

On the rare occasions when we do hire staff from different socioeconomic, cultural, religious or ethnic backgrounds, more on-boarding support is in order. We require that staff have bi-weekly check-ins with their supervisor. These check-ins are specifically aimed at classroom management and retention. We also support their learning with targeted professional development focused on trauma, implicit bias, and child development.

Short Enrollment Periods and Limited Slots

The flexibility and open-door policies we foster at MW bring in many families who have failed, for one reason or another, to get into other programs. Our families express relief (bordering on disbelief) when they find out they're allowed into a program immediately after they register their child. Many OST programs limit registration to one month at the beginning of the school year, when families are struggling to become accustomed to a new routine. Still others limit intake to a narrow age range, accepting only 5th graders or only 9th graders. This kind of setup primarily serves donors, who want to be able to track a cohort and play "savior" to a specific group of kids. It doesn't, however, help a 6th grader who learns about a program that began in 5th grade—one year too late.

Programs also reduce access by having short enrollment periods and limited student slots. Enrollment periods often can be as short as a month or two, providing parents no alternative opportunities to engage with the organization or enroll their children. It's a way that programs attempt to stay on mission while reducing the messiness of ongoing registration, attendance issues, and dealing with other challenges (often the result of trauma). Programs, in effect, are enrolling only the highly-supported youth whose parents found the program, enrolled them on time and did all the follow-up. This creates and maintains an equity gap between students who are high-need and those with adequate resources.

High-Stakes Program Requirements

OST programs often have high-stakes program requirements, such as requiring students to achieve and maintain certain grades in school, or attend several times per week. The failure to meet these requirements often results in expulsion from the program. But the more requirements, the less likely a participant coming from a troubled or traumatized family will be able to meet them. Under-resourced students whose families are distressed often find themselves in the position of caretaker for the elderly, younger children, and even sick parents. They get expelled from programs for poor attendance, but their circumstances are rarely taken into account.

We do have some program requirements at MW. Students are required to attend three or more times per week (the Mighty Academy for grades 3–8) or one time per week (Teen Scholars for grades 9–12). But MW believes that there should always be a place for youth. Families faced with barriers to attendance don't deserve to be excommunicated and cut off from a valuable resource. MW has a policy of always having something to offer these families: a shorter-term workshop with a lesser time commitment, drop-in tutoring, or writing mentorships. We train and encourage our staff to find the best fit for each family so they can stay connected.

OUTREACH STRATEGIES & RECOMMENDATIONS

In addition to those mentioned in the previous section, there are numerous strategies and recommendations that we've developed to address the challenges which, I believe, can help mitigate some of the power and resource inequities. These include training staff in trauma-informed practices, engaging staff in professional learning communities, and conducting focused and high-touch outreach.

Train Staff in Trauma-Informed Educational Practices

Training staff and volunteers who work with traumatized populations has become an important tool in the OST field. Trauma-informed education begins with learning about brain development during the ages 0–6, and how brain development is hindered in situations that evoke toxic stress. Learning about what early trauma does to the brain helps staff recognize the signs of trauma in youth and families and help them to empathize with their struggles. For example, if an adult is acting suspicious of a staff member, staff trained in trauma-informed care will not take it personally.

I had been working with a 3rd grader, Sharlene's younger sister, for two years. One day, she received a behavior consequence and lost one day of MS program time. The day she was supposed to be absent, her mother showed up furious. She stormed through our front doors into a room where 15 youth, four volunteers, and I were conducting a writing lesson.

I calmly asked her to step outside with me. I listened as she called me names, made assumptions, and defended her daughter's right to be present in my program. It was our first in-person interaction. Over the course of several minutes, I took deep breaths before I spoke. I remained calm and endeavored not to take anything she said personally. I calmly explained our behavior policies, how much I enjoyed working with her daughter, and how welcomed the child would be into the next day's program. I de-escalated the situation, but I doubted I would ever be able to explain or teach my approach to another staff member.

In my early years as a supervisor I struggled to help my staff navigate similarly difficult situations with parents. I suspect that many felt I wasn't on their side or didn't understand. Years later, trauma-informed practices gave me better language to explain and demonstrate acceptable staff responses to difficult situations.

We train all staff on trauma-informed educational principles and encourage them to give youth and parents the benefit of the doubt as often as they need it. Dr. Sandra Bloom, who developed the Sanctuary Model, a framework for developing trauma-informed, safe and constantly evolving organizations and societies, conducts one-day introductions to the model in collaboration with Michael O'Bryan at several locations in Philadelphia. Mighty Writers staff attend on an annual basis along with program staff from other organizations.

Staff who understand trauma are more likely to recruit and retain under-resourced families. They have more tools for building long-lasting, supportive relationships with families and ensure that they remain a part of the community for years to come. Both they, and the families, subsequently reap countless benefits and connections along the way.

Engage Staff in Professional Learning Communities

MW is intentional about developing a community of lifelong learners with a high level of autonomy. We support a professional learning community (PLC), a group of staff and volunteers who gather monthly during the school year and weekly during the summer to learn about topics of interest. A few recent topics include supporting youth with autism, middle school youth engagement, identifying implicit bias, and project-based learning in the writing classroom. Sometimes, outside providers lead the sessions; often, the staff themselves research and lead the sessions for their colleagues.

Our PLC has fostered youth professionals to become adept at using our curriculum and navigating the community. We often hear from our staff, especially those who have worked in traditional school environments, that they have felt infantilized and belittled in school contexts, unable to own their learning or to have any control over how to guide learning with their youth. At Mighty Writers, we give them a curriculum, budgets for materials and resources, and a general direction. Then we get out of the way. Even our part-time staffers have a very high degree of autonomy and leadership within the organization. We flood our centers with resources (new technology, high-quality printers, community partners with expertise in autism or other areas that they can access when necessary). Staff feel empowered and ready to engage with every student, no matter the student's struggles or barriers.

Focus Outreach on the Highest-Need Children and Families

While children attending private schools are welcome in all of our programs, we trust that the private school families will find us. We focus our limited time and money toward participating in block parties in our city's poorest neighborhoods, attending citywide resource fairs targeting high need families, and creating relationships with Department of Health Services professionals who can refer us to families in crisis.

At a block party or resource fair, a MW staff member might be joined by one or two volunteers and a couple of MW teen participants. They bring a branded, bright red tablecloth, and giveaway items—a MW pen, notebook, or candy. They have a handful of flyers for MW programs and engage passersby in friendly banter. Each representative is responsible for conveying the Mighty message: if kids and teens can think and write with clarity, they'll be successful at home, school, and in life. We ask potential participants to sign an email list and we immediately reach out with information on age-appropriate programs.

MW staff commit to attending back-to-school nights for at least three local schools, in order to introduce ourselves and connect to new families. At one site, MW El Futuro, where the MW Academy program fills up within a week of its announcement, we've switched to sending direct mailings written in Spanish to the Mexican community in South Philly, so that they can sign up before we send out eblasts to the community at large.

Always Answer the Question, "What's in It for Me?"

The way a program is marketed contributes significantly to early interest. We know parents are busy, so our descriptions need to be short and clear, answering the question "What's in it for me?"

Parents are the audience when you market elementary programs. Most parents want what is best for their children, and the program has to be explicit about the acquisition of literacy skills while also sounding fun and engaging. Parents desire programs that will excite their children; it doesn't help anyone if they're dragging their child, kicking and screaming, in our doors. We come up with catchy workshop titles, or hooks, such as *Winter Weather Watch* to teach prediction, *Crafty Readers* to build reading skills and *Mighty Inventors* to develop sequential writing.

One has to walk a fine line when marketing to middle schoolers. It involves marketing to parents and youth at the same time. Middle schoolers often want to express themselves in writing, and to use writing to figure out who they are in relation to others. As a result, our themes for this age group focus on identity, such as *Hip-hop 101, Sportswriting* or *My Poetic Life.* Parents have to be able to "sell" the option to their sons or daughters, since middle school students have an increasing say in their activities.

In high school, we market directly to the teens. We're competing with sports, family obligations and part-time jobs, and as a result need to tap into youth's hopes and dreams in order to connect our program to their long-term goals. Since many high schoolers are thinking about college applications, we hold programs in *College-ready Writing, Fake News,* and *Personal Narrative.*

Invest in High Touch Outreach

When youth sign up but don't show, we find out why. Families who sign up for programs but do not show are often facing the greatest challenges—parents juggling two or more jobs, combating chronic illness, or facing food or housing insecurity. We conduct high touch outreach with phone calls and ask questions such as, "Is everything ok? Is there any way we can help? How can we make sure your child will be here for our next meeting?"

We instituted a temporary "phone bank" every two weeks as a result of one particular crisis. At the time we were losing staff, and morale was low. Recruitment and retention was suffering; students weren't signing up for spring workshops. Staff didn't seem to have knowledge about the families or what was going wrong. We began calling previous program participants who no longer attended.

The results of the phone calls were powerful. Kids and parents made a personal connection with staff and were reminded that MW staff cared about their well-being and academic success. The sign-ups began rolling in. Most staff became more engaged, too, as they learned about or were reminded of the competing priorities and struggles of the families. We created a phone bank staff training—the first task was to listen to what parents had to say. The second task, if appropriate, was to sign kids and teens up for workshops. Calling families became a non-negotiable criterion for new staffers: you don't want to make phone calls? Then you don't work here.

Offer Multiple Levels of Engagement for Youth

In communities where anxiety about immigration status reigns or poverty abounds, the challenges of raising children are even greater. Programs need to make it as easy as possible for families to engage. When a family reaches out to MW for the first time, we offer them something within two weeks. To do this, we create multiple "ways in" and levels of engagement. For some, that means participating in the rigorous Mighty Academy and Teen Scholars program, which are year-long commitments. Others can participate in monthly writing workshops which involves less commitment. Another option is a series of six 90-minute sessions. Youth who sign up for this experience must attend all workshops. Finally, we offer one-time workshops such as *Comic Madness* with a visiting illustrator, or *College Essay Night*. These allow youth the flexibility to sign up for one-time or long-term opportunities based on their need, interest, and availability.

Offer Flexible Programming

Flexible programming places participants' needs at the center of all programming decisions. A flexible curriculum allows staff to listen to requests and suggestions from youth, and respond by introducing new topics and genres. For example, if an activity isn't speaking to youth, staff are equipped with a grab-bag of alternatives. Most of our writing projects are built into 6-week units, but if instructors see students losing enthusiasm for a topic, they can take a break for a week of poetry or shorten the unit.

The choice of writing project units offers instructors another opportunity to listen to youth interests and feedback. We currently have 25 curriculum units for grades 3–12, about 20 of which were developed in-house and five of which were adopted from outside partners. Instructors complete 5–6 of these units in one school year. Which units? It's entirely up to them and their participants. Promoting youth choice, the participants often vote on the next topic, theme or genre.

Finally, we create formal and informal avenues for students (and parents) to provide feedback. A month does not pass without them hearing from us via email, text, or personal inquiry asking them to assess the program.

Communicate Expectations Clearly, Early, and Often

"Why don't you charge for Mighty Writers programs?" some people ask, and go on with, "people have a difficult time understanding the value of something when it's free." This notion is condescending and inaccurate. Charging any amount of money for our programs would decrease access by eliminating the poorest families. Furthermore, parents know exactly how valuable our programs are. They know because their children attend schools where there is no soap in the bathrooms, let alone supplies in the classrooms. They come to us and see that we're well-stocked, our staff care about and are invested in youth, and we are determined to improve the quality of our offerings on an ongoing basis.

It is at times challenging to keep the value of a free program front and center. It's also difficult to help parents understand how important it is that their child shows up for each session. This can be addressed by communicating program expectations clearly, early, and often. Communicating the value of our programs and the commitment needed from each participant is key to improving access for all families.

For our time-intensive Mighty Academy, Teen Scholars, and mentorship programs, we communicate expectations in a family interview before the program begins. We review the expectations with students during the first 2–3 sessions and we schedule monthly check-ins with parents. Our short-term, once weekly, workshops are a lesser investment, but we still communicate clearly at every stage with families. When they sign up, new workshop participants receive a confirmation email. Forty-eight hours before the workshop begins, they receive a reminder email. We send out other communications via SMS and request that all families complete a survey after the workshop, even for one-time experiences.

We leverage both old and new methods of communication. Targeted email lists are a part of the secret sauce in recruitment and retention. MW's mailing list of nearly 20,000 names includes over a dozen segmented sub-lists. Some sub-lists are grouped by volunteers, teachers and community partners, kids aged 0–12, teens 13+, and more. When a site is managed well and the outreach to the community is strong, all it takes is a single eblast to fill several workshops with students.

Our email list is constantly growing, and staff and administrators at every level of the organization contribute to the lists. New participants and volunteers who sign up through our website have their information auto-loaded into our data management system. From there, we conduct monthly uploads to our eblast platform. We collect emails at every opportunity: back-to-school nights, during phone calls and when community members wander in to a program. We can't, however, rely on technology for all of our communication. Sharlene and her posse still come to MW South, but we can't reach her classmate three blocks away whose family doesn't have internet. Relationships must be cultivated and maintained through the phone calls and in-person opportunities such as family information sessions, parties and informal check-ins. In short, creating access for our highest need students means leveraging technology for communication and relationship-building and simultaneously implementing simple, old-school communication strategies.

Think Big

As we build tight-knit groups of kids, volunteers and staff in each writing center, we're simultaneously building citywide support for literacy. Our goal is to take the city from "worst to first," in literacy, and we believe we will accomplish this by partnering with like-minded organizations. In 2016, we attempted a Guinness World Record by bringing together 3,000 youth on the steps of the Philadelphia Museum of Art to write, "What I would do if I were president." We also host MightyFest, a four-day, family-friendly festival of writing which includes Mighty Writers day at over 60 branches of the Free Library of Philadelphia, a Friday night dance party, a Saturday kids' writing carnival, a Sunday morning gospel breakfast honoring Philadelphia's own Dixie Hummingbirds, and a keynote address by Nikole Hannah-Jones, an award-winning investigative reporter covering racial injustice for the *New York Times Magazine.*

Events like the World Record and MightyFest connect our young people to the larger community. Youth see city officials, radio personalities and local basketball players proclaiming importance of writing at these events. They meet other youth from all over the city who call themselves "Mighty Writers," and who may have participated in the same writing workshops. They feel connected to a broader network of support.

It's important to note that in Philadelphia, neighborhoods get a bad rap, and residents stay close to home, seldom crossing certain boundary lines. In some cases, the fear is real and based on actual events. In other cases, the fear is simply fear of the unknown. At our public events, we try to have all neighborhoods represented in positive ways. For example, at a recent event, we featured a drum line from West Philly, a dance team from Northeast Philadelphia and a young Mexican writer from South Philly.

CONCLUSION

In much of the OST world, programs reflect the baked-in inequities of our public schools among other types of systems. In many cases, the most high-quality programs target the most stable families who already have social capital and socioeconomic advantages. Underserved kids are left with the most basic programs whose highest achievement may be to simply "keep kids off the streets." These programs are usually under-resourced themselves, and struggle to provide quality services for children and youth.

When I first entered the OST profession ten years ago, the conversation was around whether ours could be a professional field with standards, high-quality research and pathways for career growth. Few research studies were conducted by, nor were articles and books written by youth development practitioners. Now, we no longer must ask if this is a professional career path. Instead, we must ask ourselves whether we wish to follow in the footsteps of our still-segregated education system and/or communities, or if we can find a better way. Building knowledge of and understanding about where we locate our OST programs and how we recruit and retain youth will offer them more opportunities to find their path to success. This is especially true for those children and youth not being served by their local public schools or other community institutions.

Sharlene, the summer after she was held back from second grade and long before she became the strong analytical and critical thinker she is today, hit the nail on the head. When it comes to a high-quality OST program, we must ask ourselves: who's it for?

How we answer that question, I believe, will determine the fate of our field.

RESEARCH CONNECTIONS FROM THE EDITORS

This chapter provides a compelling rationale for recruiting and retaining high need youth, as well as highly practical strategies for doing so. It reminds us that if we really want to focus on equity, we need to be as intentional about our outreach and retention methods as we are about designing any other program activity. Of great importance is how we communicate with and train staff about our mission, and provide tools, such as professional development, to help them with their work. Outreach and retention is not "sexy," yet critical if we want to get the young people who need services the most to cross our thresholds.

The literature is scant regarding outreach and retention of high need youth, and practice appears to be outpacing research. Indeed, most research has focused on older youth, because they are more autonomous, "vote with their feet," and an obvious challenge for programs (Deschenes, Little & Arbreton, 2010; Pelcher & Rajan, 2016). Some cities have created funding streams especially targeted to programs for older youth (e.g., New York City Department of Youth & Community Development's School's Out New York funding for grades 6–8th grade). Yet, elementary school youth can also be hard to recruit, especially if the OST program is community- or neighborhood-based rather than located in a school setting. Transportation has been identified in the literature as a major obstacle for program attendance but is only one out of many issues that keep youth away from high-quality programs (Kennedy, Wilson, Valladares & Bronte-Tinkew, 2007).

Future research needs to address how we are recruiting and retaining high need youth. Determining those who are not accessing services is as important as those who are, and probably quite daunting. Are they new immigrants with residency status issues? Are they rural youth? Rachel Loeper has also identified many systemic features, particularly those of program design (e.g. limited enrollment periods) that create obstacles and keep youth away from programs. Future research on equity needs should examine and seek to understand those systemic features that exclude high need youth as well as understand features that are working in OST programs. Finally, the chapter focused on the importance of professional development as a strategy to provide staff with skills that will help them to recruit and retain high need youth and families. One area that is emerging as a viable strategy is trauma-informed care. We need research on how this type of training impacts staff interaction with families and children. How does this professional development translate on the ground? Does it indeed have a positive impact? How can we measure and document the impact of this specialized and cross-disciplinary professional development?

REFERENCES

Borden, L. M., Perkins, D. F., Villarruel, F. A., & Stone, M. R. (2005). To participate or not to participate: That is the question. *New Directions for Youth Development, 105,* 33–49.

Borden, L. M., Perkins, D. F., Villarruel, F. S., Carleton-Hug, A., Stone, M. R., & Keith, J. G. (2006). Challenges and opportunities to Latino youth development: Increasing meaningful participation in youth development programs. *Hispanic Journal of Behavioral Sciences, 28*(2), 187–208.

Deschenes, S., Little, P., Grossman, J., & Arbreton, A. (2010). Participation over time: Keeping youth engaged from middle school to high school. *Afterschool Matters, 12*(2), 1–8.

Hall, G., Porche, M. V., Grossman, J., & Smashnaya, S. (2015). Practices and approaches of out-of-school time programs serving immigrant and refugee youth. *Journal of Youth Development, 10*(2), 72–87.

International Youth Foundation. (2016). *Mapping opportunity youth needs in the US.: A research scan.* Retrieved from https://www.iyfnet.org/sites/default/files/library/MappingOpportunityYouthNeeds_ReConnectingYouth.pdf

Kennedy, E., Wilson, B., Valladares, S., & Bronte-Tinkew, J. (2007, June). *Improving attendance and retention in out-of-school time programs* (Child Trends Research Brief No. 2007-17) Retrieved from https://www.nova.edu/projectrise/forms/improving-attendance-retention.pdf.

Lewis, K., & Burd-Sharps, S. (2015). *Zeroing in on place and race: Youth disconnection in America's cities. Measure of America of the Social Science Research Council.* Retrieved from: http://ssrc-static.s3.amazonaws.com/wp-content/uploads/2015/06/MOA-Zeroing-In-Final.pdf

Pearson, L. M., Russell, C.A., & Reisner, E. R. (2007). *Evaluation of OST programs for youth: Patterns of youth retention in OST programs.* Washington, DC: Policy Studies Associates.

Pelcher, A., & Rajan, S. (2016). After-school program implementation in urban environments: Increasing engagement among adolescent youth. *Journal of School Health, 86*(8), 585–594.

Perkins, D. F., Borden, L. M., Villarruel, F. A., Carlton-Hug, A., Stone, M. R., & Keith, J. G. (2007). Participation in structured youth programs: Why ethnic minority youth choose to participate—Or not to participate. *Youth & Society, 38*(4), 420–442.

Sanzone, J., Vaden, Y., Russell, C. St., & Sinclair, B. (2011). *Staffing and skill-building in the DYCD Out-of-school time initiative.* Washington, DC: Policy Studies Associates.

White House Council for Community Solutions. (2012). *Corporation for national and community service. Final report: Community solutions for opportunity youth.* Washington, DC: U.S. Government Printing Office.

CHAPTER 4

ROOTED IN SCARCITY AND DEFICIT

Time to Reconsider the Funding Process

Rebecca Fabiano

I've worked for, in, and with nonprofit and youth serving organizations for nearly 25 years. I currently run a small company supporting youth serving organizations and their staff. The company provides networking opportunities, professional development, and original youth programming, and I fundraise as part of my job. In addition, I serve on the board of a small foundation that provides grants to arts-based organizations in the Philadelphia area. Because of these experiences I understand both sides—the responsibility and burden of having to raise money for an organization, as well as the difficulty of selecting an organization to receive grant funds.

I am fortunate to serve on a foundation board that works hard to be thoughtful, fair, and conscientious in its giving. I give other funders the benefit of the doubt and assume they also operate similarly. Even so, I believe that the funding process, whether that of private foundations or public institutions (e.g., state or federal grants), are rooted in patriarchal, classist frameworks that keep nonprofit youth organizations operating from a poverty and scarcity mentality. It forces them to compete instead of collaborate and requires organizations to position themselves as being deficient or lacking.

Changemakers! Practitioners Advance Equity and Access in Out-of-School Time Programs,
pages 59–72.

Applying for funding can be experienced as highly paternalistic as well as administratively burdensome by social service agencies, a 'trial by fire' or hazing process. Kleinman (2017) questions why foundations don't help grantees using similar approaches to those used by venture capitalists[1] and writes, "RFPs (Request for Proposals) and funder-borne calls to serve home-grown theories of change have established an unproductive power dynamic that stunts creative problem solving with grantees, inadvertently (and almost passive-aggressively) steering their efforts. Reporting requirements and restrictions on how dollars can be used... are distracting, and even crippling." (Kleinman, 2017, p. 2). In other words, foundations, and all types of funders, need to reconsider how to support, rather than stymie, grantees. They need to help them execute and sustain their mission and vision.

In this chapter I will explore how funders view grantees from a deficit and paternalistic perspective, and how this informs the funding process. I will show how double standards are embedded in the funding process and how the myth of poverty guides the process. I believe these assumptions held by funders drive organizations, particularly those serving youth and communities experiencing trauma or which have been systemically under resourced for generations, to respond to RFPs in a problem-focused mode rather than from a position of strength. In addition, I provide recommendations for how funders can re-align themselves, through their funding process, with an asset- and strength-based view of nonprofit and youth organizations.

WHERE DO NONPROFITS GET THEIR FUNDING?

The National Center for Charitable Statistics (NCCS), a national clearinghouse of data on the nonprofit sector in the United States, identifies the following as examples of nonprofits: neighborhood associations that meet a couple of times a year, soup kitchens, and youth-serving organizations. More well-resourced nonprofit entities include the Sierra Club or the Metropolitan Opera with large budgets. All nonprofit organizations are designated a special status (501(c)(3) by the United States Internal Revenue Service.

According to scholars at NCCS, there is no "ideal" funding mix for nonprofits, rather the goal is to diversify funding sources to promote sustainability (McKeever & Pettijohn, 2014). The chart below shows the percentages of various sources of nonprofit revenue for 2014, the most current year of record. For the purposes of this chapter, I focus on the types of funding from private contributions and government grants, on which many small organizations rely for their primary sources of funding.

Figure 4.1 shows that, when combined, private contributions and government grants constitute roughly 22% of the funding that nonprofits receive. Yet, the effort needed to win those sources of income is burdensome, requiring a complex

---

[1] Venture capital is a type of private equity, a form of financing that is provided by firms or funds to small, early-stage, emerging firms that are deemed to have high growth potential, or which have demonstrated high growth (in terms of number of employees, annual revenue, or both).

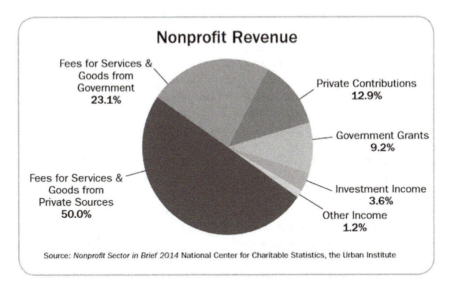

Source: *Nonprofit Sector in Brief 2014* National Center for Charitable Statistics, the Urban Institute

FIGURE 4.1

application and monitoring process. The process perpetuates a system that creates, and indeed widens, inequities. In the sections that follow, I describe this system, grouped into two categories: funding assumptions and funding structures. I close the chapter with some recommendations for funding reform.

FUNDING ASSUMPTIONS

Funders cannot give money away without a set of criteria and an application process. Public dollars must (and should) be carefully distributed and accounted for. However, the grant application process can create and/or perpetuate social inequities, particularly for organizations run by and for marginalized groups. Belief systems perpetuating inequities include paternalism, double standards, the myth of poverty, and a deficit view of nonprofits.

Paternalism

Nonprofits are viewed, and indeed treated, the way society treats poor people (Le, 2017). This may stem from "…funding and accounting practices [that] are anchored in a severe and pervasive distrust of nonprofits, the same distrust we heap on individuals with low-incomes" (Le, 2016, p. 4). Funding restrictions and strict monitoring are born out of the fear that nonprofits, like those living in poverty, will "probably waste money on fancy chairs and blinged-out business cards" (Le, 2016, p. 1). This is rank paternalism; funders are treating their grantees like disobedient children who need to be constantly watched and disciplined (Shuman, 2005).

Budgeting Double Standards

I've often gone to private funders' offices for meetings and been greeted by a well-groomed friendly receptionist, sitting in a well-lit office behind a beautiful bouquet of fresh flowers. The receptionist immediately offers me something to drink: A cup of coffee? A cup of tea? I'm then directed to a room streaming with natural light, replete with state-of-the-art technology. Bottles of water are available at every seat along with a notepad and a fancy pen. Technology is utilized if someone can't attend in person so she or he can call in or even video chat, projected on a big screen that silently glides down from a hidden compartment in the ceiling.

The irony, and double-standard, is that grant-seeking organizations are rarely allowed to request these amenities in their proposals, either in direct or overhead costs. Organizations can't include a line item for flowers in their budget. Nor can they include healthy food at their staff or board meetings. Though funders know that well-lit spaces with ergonomically correct desks and accessible technology are good for their staff, the same opportunities are generally not extended to grantees or their clients via allowable use of funds.

Funders often do not cover other vital resources that support the mission and vision of nonprofits. While private foundations typically have more flexibility than public dollars, grant applications, especially small ones, only partially cover or do not allow:

- Training or capacity building for staff, including coaching, or conference travel/attendance (generally referred to as Professional Development or PD);
- Evaluation and assessment by an external evaluator;
- Food (healthy and fresh);
- Stipends or scholarships for teens;
- Marketing and publications;
- Research and design/innovation;
- Scholarships for clients/participants/staff;
- Capital improvements to or within a building;
- Opportunities to test or try new ideas; or
- Fair wages for all staff.

These limitations may reflect a lack of trust on the part of funders that organizations will spend money wisely, or that staff and/or youth deserve the amenities in the first place. It may also reflect a lack of understanding that to run a high-quality nonprofit requires investment in human capital and ongoing capacity building.

The Myth of Poverty

Poverty is often glamorized by the wealthy. It goes hand in hand with the "pull yourself up by your bootstrap" notion that if everyone just works hard enough, they can achieve their dreams. The irony is that one can't "pull oneself up by the bootstraps." It is physically impossible. Let's imagine a recreation center on the South Side of Chicago (auto response in the brain for most will conjure images of poor black and brown kids) where the staff have "chosen" to go in on the weekends to paint motivational quotes on cinder-block walls with paint they purchased themselves. They have emptied their own closets to make sure their participants have a winter coat or asked their own family members to donate gift cards for the art supply store. This kind of story is what makes this work charming to other people. They are what make those staff "dedicated," the kids "resilient" (and worthy).

Poverty, however, is not charming. It is a grinding, critical social issue that out-of-school time programs work, indeed, struggle against. When funders are "charmed" by the actions of those living and working in poverty, this paternalism detracts from the missions of youth development organizations and undermines their struggle.

The Deficit Model

Organizations must demonstrate that they are both competent *and* in need of support in a grant application process. The latter is a deficit view of organizations that focuses on a) fixing what's "broken," b) short-term solutions, c) dependent relationships and c) reliance on expert knowledge, which, in the case of nonprofits, usually means someone external to the organization (Hamilton, Hamilton, & Pittman, 2004).

The deficit model places an emphasis on reducing risks by expecting that organizations develop more effective coping strategies and by prescribing specific supports or resources. Deficit thinking keeps the focus on the problems, rather than looking for inherent assets or strengths within an organization or community upon which can be built (Hamilton, Hamilton, & Pittman, 2004; Hammond & Zimmerman, n.d.).

If youth are viewed as a set of statistical information based in deficits (e.g., receives free lunch, attends Title One School, lives in poorest zip code in the state), then organizations are asked to operate from a 'glass half empty' framework regarding their own agency and the youth they serve. If we are using deficit language, then we are creating a deficit-focused world.

FUNDING STRUCTURES AND REQUIREMENTS

The Grant Application Process and Request for Proposals

The grant application process often takes several time-consuming steps. These include submitting a letter of interest as a way of introducing oneself to the funder and providing an overview of the work. The process might include attending a bidders' conference where the funder provides an overview of the parameters of the grant. This might happen in-person or online, via webinar. It can sometimes be difficult to contact a person at a foundation directly and often the only way to do so is by the letter of interest or the application process. Nonprofits must then draft their grant proposal; adhering to all the grant requirements including deadlines.

Navigating the grant application or request for proposal (RFP) can be challenging due to its complexity. Funders expect grantees to follow the instructions in an RFP to the letter. Some RFPs are complex—using dense and convoluted language (rarely translated into another language other than English). It needs careful reading and review to fully understand what is being asked. Nonprofits can be deterred at this early stage since limited staff time and resources do not afford sufficient time to make sense of the grant requirements. Dense and convoluted language can be particularly arduous for staff whose first language is not English. Le (2015) writes, "If your application is basically a PhD dissertation, you're perpetuating inequity (p. 1)"

Project descriptions, required by nearly all RFPs, can also present a barrier. The project description often comes with a word limit, and nonprofits may be asked to describe their plans in 500 words or less. Word limits like this constrain the ability of nonprofits to thoroughly explain their vision and goals, processes, or a theory of change. Furthermore, word counts may deter nonprofits from proposing large scale projects that will truly benefit the organization. Instead, they may propose small, straight-forward projects that may have less impact.

One caveat is that word limits do serve a purpose; they encourage writers to be concise. Due to the volume of proposals that funders receive, concise writing is a practical necessity. Yet, the need for brevity should be not outweigh a thorough understanding of a project or service. In fact, using plain language to convey grant requirements and allowing adequate space for project descriptions may improve the quality of proposals submitted to funders.

The Elusive General Operating Funds

Most funders will not fund general operating support. General operating grant funds are ones that are unrestricted—they can be used for a variety of items or activities to help an organization meet its mission or goals. For example, funds can be invested in new technologies or hiring staff, such as a part time grant writer.

Kleinman (2017) suggests that when a foundation focuses on funding projects, rather than providing general operating funds, it treats grantees as "subcontractors for a foundation's vision (p. 3)." That is, rather than supporting long-term and sustainable work, it limits support to the short-term.

Finally, as mentioned above, agencies are not allowed to request what they really need to operate effectively. This includes training or capacity building for staff, coaching, conference travel/attendance, evaluation and assessment by an external evaluator; (healthy, fresh) food; stipends for teens; scholarships for clients/participants/staff. Here, we see the budgeting double standard at work. Funders may acknowledge the utility of general operating funds but choose not to provide this kind of fiscal support. In this case, the deficit model may drive funders' thinking. That is, general operating funds do not fix a "problem," no matter how innovative the strategy.

Deadlines and Turnaround Time

In the case of public monies, RFPs are often released with too short notice for agencies to complete a detailed and sometimes lengthy grant application. As someone who regularly writes proposals and applications for funding, and is hired to write curriculum or trainings, it takes me three hours to write one hour of new content. This includes research, an outline, and first draft. For grant applications requiring a great deal of information; or even those that require you to explain your organization's "life work" in 200 words or less, the amount of time it takes to write a well-written application can easily take several hours. There is little time to gather additional information requested by funders such as letters of support and resumes. Some grant applications require signatures from board members (reflecting the lack of trust; the funder needs to be sure someone has read this and can vouch for the work). In many cases, small grassroots nonprofits do not have a dedicated, professional grant writer and Executive Directors step into this role. Executive Directors of small nonprofits wear multiple hats and their time is pulled in many directions. They are often managing human resources, finance, communications as well as fundraising which makes finding the time for grant writing difficult. For organizations where staff's primary language isn't English, these applications take on even greater obstacles and challenges.

Short turnaround times also restrict nonprofits' ability to build authentic partnerships which are critical to youth work. Funders often require in the RFP that applicants have partners (See Ken Alexander's chapter in this book). While strong partnerships are indeed a sign of quality (Huang & Dietel, 2011), it is difficult to develop authentic partners without the appropriate time, support, structure, or resources. When nonprofits are faced with a short turnaround time, what often happens is that organizations call one another and ask if they can write them into their grant as a partner and then work out the details later. And it is not clear that this takes place. This is not the authentic partnerships that funders seek, nor ones that can bring resources and enhance agency work in meaningful, intentional, mutually-beneficial ways.

The expectation that nonprofits can overcome short deadlines and quick turnarounds on limited time and resources is reminiscent of the myth of poverty; that is, if nonprofits work hard enough they can successfully complete and win grant applications regardless of the constraints. Some funders require nonprofits to re-apply annually for grants. This is a major burden for many organizations, especially small ones with limited capacity. Re-application requires grantees to jump through hoops year after year. Executive directors and project directors are forced to spend time traveling to meet with the program officer, redoing the budget, filling out forms, and submitting a final report (Shuman, 2005).

Monitoring and Evaluation

Like the application process, some funders want multi-page, multi-attachment quarterly reports on how money is being spent. This requirement is the epitome of paternalism. The quarterly reports help funders keep a watchful eye on how organizations use grant funds. Much like the burden the application process places on nonprofits, onerous quarterly reports take staff away from the work the funding is supposed to support,their work with children and youth. This is particularly true for organizations with limited staff capacity. While it is important to report how funds are being used and the progress being made, the demands of the reporting process need not be overwhelming.

In addition to quarterly reports, nearly all RFPs include the question, "How are you going to assess your success?" Rest assured, most people in organizations are thinking about this question. In some cases, an organization will develop a quick satisfaction survey and hope for enough affirmative answers to put in their final report to the funder. Given the accountability era in which we live, evaluation seems inevitable, yet, nonprofits feel extraordinary pressure to demonstrate how much of the "problem" they have solved. Instead, the evaluation mandate should acknowledge that noticeable improvements take time. In addition, a comprehensive, quality evaluation needed to document change requires a high level of skill and knowledge rarely possessed by staff at small nonprofits. Unfortunately, hiring an external evaluator can be prohibitively expensive, and, as mentioned, it is excluded as a line item in many proposal budgets. Rather than frame evaluations as proof that a deficit is being addressed, funders need to understand that evaluation is an ongoing, iterative process that helps drive decisions about program design and program improvements.

SUGGESTIONS AND RECOMMENDATIONS

The assumptions that create inequalities are widespread and no single recommendation will change current funding trends. However, many private foundations have begun to look at their grant application processes through an equity lens and have started to adjust their grant procedures. Below, I introduce trust-based philanthropy as an alternative. I also offer specific strategies that can help to reform the funding process and procedures.

Trust-based philanthropy

The Whitman Institute believes that philanthropy can be more effective when funders approach their grantee relationships from a place of trust, rather than suspicion. They have developed a framework, entitled the *Nine pillars of a trust-based philanthropy* (https://thewhitmaninstitute.org/). The following are the foundations that guide this approach to funding:

1. *Provide Unrestricted, Multi-Year Funding*: This allows organizations to focus on their mission without having to identify specific projects and supports the overall health of the organization. Unrestricted funding also encourages the freedom to learn, adapt, and take risks. It is critical in supporting an organization's sustainability and effectiveness.

2. *We Do the Homework*: Funders take responsibility for getting to know the organization, the issue(s) that the organization is proposing to address and the organization's assets. The burden of proof in determining whether a leader and organization is a good fit is on the funder.

3. *Partner in the Spirit of Service*: Funders understand and respect the knowledge of the organization and can place themselves shoulder to shoulder, not ahead of, the grantee as everyone learns, together.

4. *Offer Open and Responsive Communication*: Funders have an 'open door' policy and don't rely on quarterly reports for updates from grantees. Instead, they spend time getting to know the organization and establish ongoing, regular, respectful, and helpful communication.

5. *Solicit and Act on Feedback*: Funders regularly solicit, reflect on, and take action on feedback from grantees.

6. *Encourage Transparency*: Funders recognize that the work of nonprofits may be evolving and make room for course corrections or innovations without fear of negative consequences. This encourages organizations to take reasonable risks and to innovate without fear of losing funding.

7. *Simplify and Streamline Paperwork*: By reducing the amount of paperwork, funders allow grantees more time to focus on their work, as opposed to the paperwork. One way to streamline paperwork is for funders to adopt a shared/common application.

8. *Support Beyond the Check*: Funders consider other ways to support grantees. This could include making introductions to influential others or facilitating effective partnerships or providing capacity building for board members or staff. It might even mean highlighting an organization's leadership and work; being a sounding board and source of advice; or providing spaces for reflection, connecting, and convening.

9. *Host Restorative Retreats*: Funders allow time for restoration; organizations that work with individuals or communities that have experienced trauma need time to reflect, reconnect, and recommit to the work.

Funders, both private and public, may not be able to immediately move towards implementing all nine pillars, but they can make intentional efforts to integrate some of these ideals into their processes and procedures.

Modifications to Grantmaking Processes

Based on my research and experience, I believe that there are other modifications that can help funders address inequality and become more strength-based.

Trying even one of the recommendations could signal to grantees that funders are attempting to make their experience less burdensome and provide a more equitable application experience.

Use the Common Application. The National Network of Grantmaking has urged funders to adopt a short, common application form, which would greatly cut down on grantee paperwork. The common application can streamline the grant-seeking process so that organizations can adapt one application for multiple funders. Another benefit of a common application is that it can be used to gather important data about applicants and the needs of grantees. This information will help inform funders' interactions with grantees and how they go about writing RFPs for the next round of grants. A collective effort by a group of regionally based foundations to inform and encourage the use of the common application would increase access for organizations. Affinity-based groups of funders, such as the Youth Advocacy Funders Group and Grantmakers for Education, can also pool and target resources.

Use Asset-Based Language in RFPs. The language of the RFP can be changed to be more aligned with an asset-based framework. Some examples of asset-based questions on a RFP include:

- What is your vision for the work?
- What is your organization currently working on that contributes to this vision?
- What community resources are available to help enact this vision?
- What support would you need to leverage these resources?

Kleinman (2017) suggests that funders, rather than asking organizations to describe a project, ask potential grantees to focus on supporting individuals. For example, an application could ask an organization to introduce the most interesting, compelling, or resilient participants. Indeed, in the international development arena, videos of grantees talking about their hopes, dreams, and accomplishments or demonstrating the impact of the grant (such as a well to supply clean water to a community) has become a quite common aspect of the application process or grant report. In other words, the RFP could ask potential grantees to describe participants' talents, dreams and aspirations and how the funding could, and has, helped them achieve those dreams. Strength-based language allow organizations to write from a perspective of possibility and encourages them to focus less on problems and more on solutions. Indeed, an emphasis on strengths is more in line with positive philosophy undergirding much of the social work and youth development fields.

Match Funding Cycles to Programs' Schedule. Funders, when writing an RFP, could consider the natural calendar of events for nonprofits. Youth-serving organizations for example, have a predictable rhythm to their work. Work moves quickly and is most intense from May to the end of August with an uptick at the beginning of the school year. Things slow down between the Christmas holiday and the beginning of February. The workload is moderate from March to May. If funders learn about their grantees and events that influence their calendars, it could reduce stress for applicants. This could include timing the proposal's due date during the slower months. Open ended and rolling applications are also helpful, especially for organizations with limited capacity.

Support Data Informed Program Improvement. Rarely are there questions in a proposal about how formative evaluation and assessment are going to drive the project, or how the data will be used after it's been collected. Rather than measure outcomes, the evaluation section of RFPs might include questions that encourage data-informed modifications such as: What do you hope to learn and how will you know if you learn it? What will success look like at the different phases of this work? How are you defining quality and how will you measure it?

Facilitate Funding Pathways. As part of the reapplication process, funders could work with other funders to 'pass off' an organization as it moves to another stage of the work or reached a particular outcome, to a funder more aligned with that 'stage.' Perhaps an evaluation framework or set of criteria that would track an organization as it improves in quality could guide this process. To successfully "pass off" an organization, funders would need to replace short-term funding with a funding continuum based on success, agency growth, and constituents' needs.

CONCLUSION

The good news is that many funders are moving towards more strengths-based, more equitable, and less cumbersome approaches to funding social service and the work of nonprofits. For example, the New York Women's Foundation, in a major break with paternalistic approaches to funding, explicitly stating that they practice "participatory grantmaking. Guidance for grantmaking comes directly from the communities to be supported, and grantmaking is principally carried out by volunteer activists" (New York Women's Foundation, n.d.).

For funders who aren't quite there yet, and aspire to move in this direction, they must look at their current practices and consider making significant shifts in their philosophies and approaches to grantees. This chapter offers a few strategies that can make a real difference. Unfortunately, it is not as simple as adopting new policies and procedures. The assumptions, such as a deficit view of communities, have led funders to institutionalize current funding practices and are pervasive, deeply rooted, and historical. Questioning those assumptions and uncovering additional assumptions underlying the established funding processes will likely reveal additional ways to improve access to much needed financial support.

Non-profits, for their part, must seek opportunities to educate and help funders understand when and how the funding process is experienced as being deficit-focused, unduly burdensome, and paternalistic. Of course, this can be a delicate matter to approach with a funder because they ultimately hold the purse-strings.

Building a strong relationship with program officers is a start. This includes sharing your organization's work—successes, challenges, goals, and aspirations—early and often. Invite funders to events such as festivals, art shows, and other types of demonstrations of the organization's good work. During these celebrations, there will be opportunities to slip in discussions about the constraints and burdens that the funding process place on the organization.

Funders and nonprofits should not lose sight of their common interest; to provide quality services to children, youth, and their families. Working side-by-side with one another to overhaul the funding system will have a major impact.

RESEARCH CONNECTIONS FROM THE EDITORS

The topic of how funders can improve the grant process is as refreshing as it is bold. There is an inherent power imbalance in the funder—grantee relationship which can make it difficult for grantees, who need funds to keep much needed services available to youth and their families, to provide valuable feedback to funders. From the unique perspective of both funder and grantee, Rebecca Fabiano has articulated the major issues, provided compelling feedback as well as practical suggestions. She provides a rousing and honest discussion of the beliefs that undergird the funding process, and which perpetuate inequity.

The research on diversity suggests that giving people a shared, meaningful goal to work toward often disrupts prior beliefs, especially when power is shared amongst members of the team (Cohen & Lotan, 1995; Wells, Fox, & Cordova-Cobo, 2016). Future research should explore how funders and grantees can work together to collectively revise the funding process. One such study might be the impact of the participatory funding approach practiced by the New York Women's Foundation. More participatory forms of research, such as developmental evaluation provides another promising avenue. In developmental evaluation researchers collect and analyze real-time data to inform an ongoing cycle of design, development, and implementation (Patton, 2010). The method is particularly suited for testing changes to systems like the funding process and for shaping unique solutions (Parkhurst, Preskill, Lynn, & Moore, 2016).

While Fabiano recommends actions that funders can take to improve the existing funding process, there may be other concerns that can, and should, be addressed by research. Researchers can explore foundational questions such as: 1) How do grantees and funders experience the funding process? 2) What policies and procedures support grantees during the funding process? and; 3) What policies and procedures hinder grantees during the funding process? Human-centered design, typically used for creating innovative products, is another method that can be used to help answer these types of questions. Human centered design is a problem-solving method that requires deeply understanding the problem by focusing on the experience of the individuals that are affected (IDEO, n.d.). This can be done through observation, interviews or any method that provides rich detail on the experience of people. Once the problem is deeply understood, solutions can be applied. The perspective of funders, as designers of RFPs, and grantees, as applicants, will be necessary to identify unknown issues and to inform change. Before any of these changes occur, some courageous conversations must take place. Perhaps, this chapter can be a starting point.

REFERENCES

Cohen, E. G., & Lotan, R. A. (1995). Producing equal-status interaction in the heterogeneous classroom. *American Educational Research Journal, 32,* 99–120.

Grant Makers for Effective Organizations. (2014). *What is general operating support and why is it important? The smarter grantmaking playbook.* Retrieved from https://www.geofunders.org/resources/what-is-general-operating-support-and-why-is-it-important-678.

Hamilton, S. F., Hamilton, M. A., & Pittman, K. (2004). *Principles for youth development. The youth development handbook: Coming of age in American communities* (Vol. 2, pp. 3–22).

Hammond, W., & Zimmerman, R. (n.d.). *A strengths-based perspective.* Retrieved from https://www.esd.ca/Programs/Resiliency/Documents/RSL_STRENGTH_BASED_PERSPECTIVE.pdf

Huang, D., & Dietel, R. (2011). *Making afterschool programs better* (CRESST Policy Brief No. 11). Los Angeles: University of California, Los Angeles, National Center for Research on Evaluation, Standards, and Student Testing (CRESST).

IDEO. (n.d.). *What is human-centered design?* Retrieved from http://www.designkit.org/human-centered-design

Kleinman, G. (2017). *Why aren't foundations helping their grantees like VCs?* NewCo Shift. Retrieved from https://shift.newco.co/why-arent-foundations-actually-helping-their-grantees-like-vcs-77d4437648

Le, V. (2015). *Funders, your grant application process may be perpetuating inequity.* Retrieved from: http://nonprofitaf.com/2015/08/funders-your-grant-application-process-may-be-perpetuating-inequity/.

Le, V. (2016). *We need to stop treating nonprofits the way society treats poor people.* Retrieved from http://nonprofitwithballs.com/2016/07/we-need-to-stop-treating-nonprofits-the-way-society-treats-poor-people/.

Le, V. (2017). *Progressive funders, you may be part of the problem.* Retrieved from http://nonprofitaf.com/category/fundraising-2/.

McKeever, B. S., & Pettijohn, S. L. (2014). *The nonprofit sector in brief 2014.* Washington, DC: Urban Institute. Retrieved from https://www.urban.org/sites/default/files/publication/33711/413277-The-Nonprofit-Sector-in-Brief--.PDF

Parkhurst, M., Preskill, H., Lynn, J., & Moore, M. (2016). *The case for developmental evaluation.* Retrieved from https://www.fsg.org/blog/case-developmental-evaluation.

Patton, M. Q. (2010). *Developmental evaluation: Applying complexity concepts to enhance innovation and use*. New York, NY: Guilford Press.

Shuman, M. (2005). *Why do progressive foundations give too little to too many?* Retrieved from https://www.tni.org/es/node/7388.

The New York Women's Foundation. (n.d.). *Grantmaking approach*. Retrieved from https://www.nywf.org/our-work/grantmaking-approach/

The Whitman Institute. (n.d.). *Trust-based philanthropy*. Retrieved from https://thewhitmaninstitute.org/wp-content/uploads/Trust-Based-Philanthropy-2-pager.pdf.

Wells, A., Fox, L., & Cordova-Cobo, D. (2016). *How racially diverse schools and classrooms benefit all students*. Retrieved from https://tcfdotorg.atavist.com/how-racially-diverse-schools-and-classrooms-can-benefit-all-students

WHAT DOES IT TAKE TO PROVIDE DISABLED YOUTH ACCESS TO OUT-OF-SCHOOL TIME PROGRAMS?

Suzanne Stolz

When I interviewed straight out of college to work in AmeriCorps service for a youth mentoring program, I smiled when the interviewer asked about my experience with diversity. I grew up in the Midwest, just outside of a predominately white town and was now living in a large city in California. "Having grown up with a disability," I said, "I was diversity in my hometown. I'm excited to learn more."

Little did I know that the position would lead me on a path of new discovery about diversity and disability access in out-of-school time (OST) programs and schools. Now, as a disability studies scholar with previous work experience in mentoring programs, afterschool programs, and community recreation programs, I am interested in the experience of parents, youth, and OST providers in relation to how disability access is navigated in these spaces. In this chapter, I share some of my own experiences as I explore the perspectives of these groups, outline the basic legal requirements of the ADA in relation to OST programs, discuss the

Changemakers! Practitioners Advance Equity and Access in Out-of-School Time Programs,
pages 73–90.

qualities of integrated and segregated[1] programs, and finally describe what it takes to provide a strong inclusive program.

It's important to note the language I am intentionally using throughout this chapter. I use the term "nondisabled" as it centers the experience of disability. I reject terms like "able-bodied" and "normal" as I view my own body as able and not abnormal. In addition, I intentionally use "disabled children" rather than "children with disabilities" because I myself identify as a "disabled woman." Although many educators have been taught to use person-first language, like "people with disabilities," many activists and scholars choose identity-first language as a way to illustrate that there is no shame in this part of our identity. This choice is also rooted in an understanding that we are disabled by inflexible environments and social practices that exclude us. As language is continually shifting, I encourage people to have conversations about disability-related language and be respectful of various preferences.

DISABILITY ACCESS IN OST PROGRAMS

Although I was a member of my hometown 4-H Club as a child, my parents would not send me to the 4-H Camp that my non-disabled siblings and classmates attended at Rock Springs Ranch. I didn't have the balance to stand alone independently and needed assistance putting on my leg braces and shoes. Even as a 10-year-old, I thought it was unfair. Instead, they sent me to MDA (Muscular Dystrophy Association) Camp where I would have one-on-one attention from a volunteer camp counselor and interact with other children with similar impairments. Like many parents of disabled children (Schleien, Miller, Walton, & Pruett, 2014), my parents wanted me to be involved in OST programs, but did not find sufficient access to the programs typical children attended.

With an eye on disability access, we want to consider both the likelihood of participation and the quality of participation. A 2009 study of 43,000 children investigated the factors that impacted participation in OST programs and found that disability was a factor. Twice as many physically disabled children were non-participants (Bandy & Moore, 2009). For those who participated, what was the quality of their experience? Unfortunately, some programs do not provide meaningful or equitable opportunities for participation. For example, we hear stories of disabled youth who serve as "managers" or "waterboys" for youth sports teams shared more often than stories about the contributions made by disabled athletes on the field. While this may be a valuable experience for some, it keeps disability on the sidelines and provides limited space for growth. Often, a lack of programming designed to include disability diversity limits disabled youths' options and does not appeal to their interest, yet, the law requires programs to make modifications that support disabled youths' involvement.

---

[1] Solis (2006) notes differences between imposed segregation and chosen segregation. This paper refers to both as forms of segregation.

WHAT DOES THE LAW SAY ABOUT ACCESS?

Many times overturned in US courts, the ideology of separate but equal is usually conceptualized in terms of race. But this rationalization of segregation, which still lingers within many communities, has also left many with disabilities in spaces that are separate and far from equal. Even with special education's noble goal of educating disabled students, disability studies scholars assert that special education has been a tool for maintaining racial segregation in schools (Annamma, Ferri, & Connor, 2018; Beretan, 2008; Ferri & Connor, 2005). As our history shows, what is legal and what is standard is not always equitable or ethical. As those who seek equity and justice, we can work to understand legislation and question how it compares to our ethical codes. The legacy of special education, a system that perpetuates separation, leaks into all aspects of our communities including OST youth programs and can cause staff to ask, "Isn't there a program better suited for your child and her needs?"

Title III of the Americans with Disabilities Act (ADA), signed into law in 1990, "prohibits discrimination on the basis of disability in the activities of places of public accommodations" (Information and Technical Assistance on the Americans with Disabilities Act, 2018). Places of public accommodation include schools, afterschool programs, daycare centers, and recreation facilities, including those that are privately operated. The law requires integrated settings, the maintenance of accessible features, and the modification of policies, practices, and procedures that impact access to participation. An example of a modification of policy at swimming pools is removing the prohibition of flotation devices, which without, some individuals are excluded. Programs are not allowed to use eligibility requirements that screen out individuals with any class of disability. With this, preschools and camps have had to amend expectations that children must be potty trained and able to sit still for a specific length of time. Title III of the ADA also calls for the removal of physical and communicative barriers, tolerance and space for mobility devices and service animals, and inclusion in transportation provided by public accommodations. This means a program that transports youth from school to a recreation club may need to ensure that accessible vans or buses are available (Nondiscrimination on the Basis of Disability, 1991).

Disability rights advocates point to the fact that while the ADA has been in place for nearly thirty years, violations are common and continue to impact the ability of individuals and families to access resources (Pearson, 2018). For example, a 2015 survey of 61 community youth fitness programs showed that nearly 25% lacked wheelchair accessibility and 90% lacked requirements for staff to learn how to support disabled participants (Wiart, Darrah, Kelly, & Legg, 2015). Despite legal violations to the ADA and a history of disability segregation, many youth program leaders and parents are advocating for access in OST programs. The result is two very different OST options for disabled youth, integrated programs and disability-specific programs.

THE BENEFITS OF INTEGRATED PROGRAMS
AND DISABILITY-SPECIFIC PROGRAMS

As an advocate and trainer for inclusive OST programs several years ago, I worked to help program staff understand the benefits of inclusion and build capacity for it. With experience as a child participant and an adult employee of disability-specific programs, I know it is important to also consider what benefits segregated programs offer and why so many disabled youth still attend (Mullins, 2015), and then advocate for those that serve the purpose of equity and community. It's worth exploring the questions, "What is different about integrated and segregated programs?" and "Should all youth programs be integrated?"

Integrated Programs

I mentioned above my participation in 4-H. Although I did not go to camp with children from my hometown, I was otherwise included in club meetings and activities, allowed to sign up for crafts, photography, and cooking classes. Local parents who organized these activities knew my parents, welcomed me, and offered support when I needed it. In this space, I felt a sense of belonging even while remaining a somewhat quiet, and peripheral participant.

The value of integrated programs is extensive and cannot be denied. A review of inclusive OST programs with a range of age groups found positive outcomes for disabled individuals in building social skills, developing physical strength, and maintaining psychological well-being (Arbour-Nicitopoulos et al., 2018). Because proximity is a factor in developing relationships, integrated programs can increase connections by giving access to a wider range of neighborhood peers and parents. In integrated settings, I learned as a child how to negotiate differences, how to respond to peers' questions, and how to ask for help. These skills have been integral in living, studying, and working in integrated communities, schools, and workplaces. Having the choice to participate in activities close to home is useful in giving youth a sense of belonging and practice in navigating spaces that are not necessarily designed for them. While we often point to what is added to a child's experience with access to inclusive programs, it's perhaps more important to note the impact when children encounter spaces that are "not for you."

While Arbour-Nicitopoulos et al. (2018) considered the effects of inclusive programs on disabled individuals, others have studied the effects on the general population. Although many argue that inclusion of disabled children in schools adversely affects nondisabled children, large-scale studies have found no evidence to support the claim (Ruijs, Van der Veen, & Peetsma, 2010). Others suggest that inclusive programs are beneficial for the growth of nondisabled children as well and for the promotion of inclusive communities (Odom, Buysee, & Soukakou, 2011; Sapon-Shevin, 2010). Nondisabled children engage in activities, make friends, and become comfortable with disability as children, making them less likely to be fearful as adults and more likely to navigate differences effectively.

Experience of Disabled Youth

Even in integrated programs, disabled youth can feel excluded. In general, disabled youth report having fewer friends and being victimized by bullies (Koster, Pijl, Nakken, & Van Houten, 2010; Lindsay, McPherson, Aslam, McKeever, & Wright, 2012). As a result, disabled children (Hamilton, 2005; Krull, Wilbert, & Hennemann, 2014) and teens (Symes & Humphrey, 2010) experience loneliness and can have difficulty initiating and maintaining friendship (Taylor & Houghton, 2008). However, the reality of social exclusion is not only negotiated only at a peer level, but also between youth and adults. The following are some examples:

- Several years ago, when I was working as an inclusion specialist, I shadowed a six-year-old boy while he participated in a summer program. The staff had given him a picture schedule that he could use to check off activities and have a better understanding of what was happening throughout the day. Holding the schedule, he timidly joined a group of children for a circle time sing-along and began to smile and sing. During a break between songs, another child pointed at the schedule and said, "Why does he have that?" When the staff song leader did not answer, the child pushed, "Why does he have that?" Other children turned to look at the boy. His face dropped and his head went down to hide. The leader heard the questions and did not answer.
- At another program, a thirteen-year-old girl reported being harassed by a boy. Her father shrugged and said, "She sometimes misunderstands things. We can let it go." Seeing the girl's distress, a staff member stepped in and assured everyone that the report would be taken seriously and that they would take measures to ensure that it would not happen again.

These are two examples where disabled youth encounter situations in inclusive programs[2] in which others make some statement about disability that impacts their social experience. In the first situation, the staff member likely was unsure how to talk to children about differences and how visual supports can be useful. Her failure to answer the question exemplifies the way silence around disability adds to the stigmatization of those who appear different. In the second situation, disability is almost used as a way to dismiss the girl's report. The staff member who intervened supported the girl in validating her as a trustworthy source. Although I expect these small snapshots and others create unique and memorable experiences for those navigating access, some researchers have considered overall satisfaction. One study compared the experiences of disabled and nondisabled youth in recreational services and found disabled youth were significantly less

---

[2] In this paper, I consider inclusive programs to be those which make an effort to provide disability access in an integrated setting. Of course, we can always question how much access is afforded; but, working toward this goal deserves acknowledgment. Inclusion is a process that will need ongoing effort.

satisfied. They reported a desire for better inclusion, information, and disability awareness (Magill-Evans, Darrah, & Adkins, 2003).

Disability-Specific Programs

The segregated nature of disability-specific programs troubles some individuals and their families (Mayer & Anderson, 2014; Stumbo, Wang, & Pegg, 2011) as they often want to have the choice to join friends and family members in inclusive programs (Thompson & Emira, 2011). However, there are benefits to segregated programs. In the same way that there are benefits to all-girls schools and historically black colleges, disability-specific programs have a number of benefits that are hard to match. For many disabled individuals and their families, disability-specific programs can provide a break from the harsh realities of ableism in other environments (Solis, 2006). For families who spend a great deal of time advocating in other arenas, these programs offer respite when they lack the energy to advocate more. Many integrated programs still use facilities that sorely need renovation (Mullins, 2015), while disability-specific programs usually operate in carefully-selected locations where participants more-or-less can expect physical accessibility.

A decade ago, I helped run a mentoring program in which disabled teens were matched with disabled adult mentors. One aspect of the program involved inviting disabled teens to have a "college experience," living in dorms for four days and participating in various workshops that addressed topics related to the transition out of high school. To provide access, we hired skilled care attendants to assist participants. A mother described why she thought her son could not attend. "No way. He can't get out of bed or get dressed without help." I assured her that I understood and that he could participate. For her son and several others, this was the first time they stayed overnight away from their parents and the first opportunity they had to direct their own care.

At an event leading up to the dorm stay, we held meetings for parents and youth in separate rooms and provided lunch. Another mother moved to leave the parent room, explaining, "Those are enchiladas, and she can't cut those!" I assured her that attendants would help her daughter. For both mothers, the program's accessibility was a surprise and a rare gift. Balancing social participation with the need for safety, these parents, like many, considered the supports and accommodations available before leaving their children in the care of program providers (Mullins, 2015).

Aside from easy accessibility, most disability-specific programs provide youth connections and community with others who have similar experience. Being surrounded by others who share common experiences of exclusion and who do not question your existence in the group can positively transform the way you see yourself. When I went to camp, one that specifically served disabled individuals, I felt a sense of belonging there that was different than what I felt at 4-H meetings. I could have an active role in *all* of the activities. I could be a leader. My perspective was valued. My peers at camp and I talked about the way people interacted with us in our home communities and shared our strategies for handling uncomfortable situations. Similarly, we worked together to negotiate interactions with program staff and volunteers when we felt we were treated condescendingly or with too much surveillance. As an adult, I've analyzed the complexity of the environment where I found my first disability community and survived the patronization of a cure charity[3] (Stolz, 2016). My home community and the 4-H Club lacked disabled role models that I could learn from; finding role models and peer support at camp was consequential. The following are some strategies that have been generated by this particular model.

Mentoring in Disability-Specific Programs.

Mentoring is a widely accepted strategy for supporting positive youth development (Rhodes & DuBois, 2008); and, the quality of the mentoring relationship can have significant influence on the extent of benefit. Pairing disabled mentees with disabled mentors has been found to be especially promising (Hayes & Balcazar, 2008; Morris, Fletcher-Smith, & Radford, 2017). This is not to say nondisabled mentors are not valuable, but this pairing may not be as impactful because nondisabled adults may find it more difficult to give advice on developmental hurdles that are quite different from their own experiences and disabled youth may be reluctant to share with those whose experience has been markedly different. Although integrated programs can offer mentoring, it is often more readily available in segregated, disability-specific programs. Peer mentoring was a crucial component in both of the programs I discussed above: MDA Camp where it happened informally and the mentoring program where it was intentional. Although the mentoring program ended ten years ago, the community members it brought together still support each other by sharing disability-related resources.

Matching Programs to Disabled Youths' Needs

Inclusive OST programs can unite everyone and yet, we have a ways to go in ensuring that, in integrated spaces, disabled children will find the support and accommodation they need. Until then, disability-specific programs can be crucial in providing respite from the constant need for advocacy on one's behalf, and offer resourceful connections. At this point, individuals and families want both options (Mullins, 2015). They, like any non-disabled youth, want to be offered choice in recreation.

---

[3] The Muscular Dystrophy Association (MDA) is considered by disability studies scholars to be a cure charity in that it's largest efforts go to raising money to research cures. The organization has been known to perpetuate overwhelmingly medical model views of disability through the broadcast of its annual telethon that aired from 1966 to 2010, illustrating our lives to be very limited as Jerry Lewis, the host, called our wheelchairs "steel imprisonments," rather than acknowledging the liberty wheelchairs afford us.

Interacting with a wide range of disabled youth, I have met many parents, some whom assumed that their child's impairment precluded them from getting involved outside of family activities and others who have sought access to OST programs for their children and faced challenges leading to frustration and isolation. Parents have acknowledged the difficulty in decision-making about what would be best for their children, integration or segregation, as they have noticed that others do not always anticipate their children's needs (Piškur et al., 2016). When I worked for a disability-specific mentoring program one mother illustrated her loss of trust in integrated settings. As we met to discuss her sixteen-year-old son's potential participation in the program, the woman blurted, "I am only here because you all are disabled." The young man made eye contact with each of us and then looked down as his mother described reasons she didn't trust most people with him, including an incident of abuse by someone hired by the school to help him.

A lack of adequate information about a program provider's knowledge and openness to inclusion and accommodation raises questions for parents about whether their children will be welcomed and cared for. If parents know they can request accommodations, they may have to ask an inexperienced staff member for help. Parents encounter time-consuming, bureaucratic procedures to get modified equipment and support or encounter criteria that excludes their children. Some parents make strategic connections with staff members to win access, while others now reach out via social media to find resources (Piškur et al., 2016).

Parents know their children need support to participate and wonder who will provide that support. Some jump in to provide the support when staff will not. Some encounter negative attitudes from the community (Wiart, Darrah, Kelly, & Legg, 2015). They wonder if their child will be left out and if their child will be safe (Schleien et al., 2014). When they do find a program, transportation can be a barrier (Magill-Evans, Darrah, & Adkins, 2003). That which is provided to the general population may not be accessible to those using wheelchairs and other assistance devices or those who need more supervision. Families without their own transportation often rely on school-provided transport which can limit access to activities outside of the school day.

Overall, parents tend to notice the lack of access to public spaces, schools, restrooms, and sidewalks and a lack of choice in the designs of clothing and everyday tools that are not created with their children in mind. Faced with limited options, parents often become problem-solvers (Piškur et al, 2016) and give support to staff who are not prepared to work with disabled youth. Interestingly, parents' concerns are largely related to changeable sociocultural and environmental barriers, as they counter the pervasive medical model meanings of disability (Lalvani & Polvere, 2013) which imply their children are not able to participate.

RECOMMENDATIONS FOR PROVIDING QUALITY ACCESS

Include Us at the Table

The phrase "Nothing about us, without us" has been used in disability activism since the 1990s (Charlton, 1998) as a way to remind policymakers and organizational leaders that disabled folks should always be invited to the table. Who better understands disability exclusion and disability access? As we consider improving access in OST programs, planning with disabled individuals and their families is key to making real progress. This work will be an ongoing endeavor as we start where we are, assess what is needed, make changes, and keep learning. A number of national and state organizations have created resources, toolkits, and professional development materials that highlight best practices for inclusive programs. Four high quality standards can be used to frame program practices. They include: an inclusive philosophy; inclusion strategies; an evaluation cycle; and, community outreach (Special Needs Inclusion Project, 2010). The following is a description of each of the strategies.

Inclusive Philosophy

Our philosophy about disability greatly impacts the way we interact with disabled children and their families. Do we view disability as a problem or as a natural aspect of humanity? Are people disabled by the limits of their bodies and minds or by the physical and social barriers in their environments? Our answers to these questions represent two different models of thinking about disability. The medical model, which has been historically prevalent, calls bodies and minds into question, claiming them to be deficient, abnormal, and in need of cure or rehabilitation. The social model, often adopted by activists, points to the lack of access afforded to those with natural differences and calls for changes to the environment. Scholars have acknowledged that both of these models and others are intertwined in the reality of disabled people's lives and have found parents to use both models when advocating for change (Manago, Davis, & Goar, 2017). Within the OST field, we are called to take a strength-based approach in supporting all children (Mahoney & Haley-Mize, 2017). Framing disability socially is a means to articulating a strength-based philosophy, centering cultural aspects of providing disability access, and improving the experience of disabled children in our programs.

A program's inclusion philosophy must be apparent in mission and vision statements and in written policy guides. Only then can this philosophy be intentionally implemented by administrators and program staff and reflected in strategies used to support inclusion. Quality programs review, revise, and ensure alignment of the philosophy within various aspects of the program.

Inclusion Strategies

The inclusion strategies we use are meaningful and impactful to disabled children's experience in OST programs. Of course, this means program staff likely need professional development to learn beneficial strategies. Researchers suggest that programs hire people who are open to diversity and continuous learning (Sharp, Rodas, & Sadovnik, 2012), characteristics needed for identifying children's assets, interests, and needs, and to create activities that are responsive. In building a diverse staff, programs can also consider disability as an asset and welcome disabled applicants.

In providing professional development in OST programs for several years, I found that providers' most common request was for strategies managing challenging behavior. Some of the simplistic views of behaviorism fail to teach that behavior is personal and contextual (Kluth, 2010). In developing more nuanced understandings of behavior and human diversity, providers can draw on a wide variety of tools learn to support positive behavior. Advance planning and additional support can sometimes prevent behavior challenges that happen when youth are unclear of expectations or when they are distressed by a changing environment. Visual schedules, visual supports, and social stories can be used to help children process what is happening during the day. Providers can also create socio-emotional learning opportunities that help children learn to cope with their feelings, manage their behavior, and interact effectively with others. While schedules and socio-emotional learning are markers of quality programming for everyone, specific considerations for access (i.e. making schedules visual) can be shared in inclusion resource binders or handbooks and used to benefit disabled and nondisabled participants.

Because a lack of program structure and predictability is uncomfortable for many autistic children (Brewster & Coleyshaw, 2011) and for those who experience anxiety, providers can carefully build in elements of consistency and routine to support those who struggle with unpredictable changes. In considering program structures, researchers again emphasize the power of strength-based approaches that hone in on a group's common interests and goals, promote both cooperative and individualized learning opportunities, and offer challenge in developmentally appropriate ways (Arbour-Nicitopoulos et al., 2018). In short, programs can hold high expectations for youth while employing flexible supports.

As programs commit to using culturally-responsive curriculum, providers can consider disability as a cultural aspect of children's identities (Baglieri, 2012). When we read books or watch movies together, do we question the implicit and explicit messages about disability? Do we choose positive disability representations to share? Can we learn together about the contributions of disabled people in our world? Do we invite disabled community members to share their knowledge or their stories? Having adult role models who understand a child's experience and can offer mentorship is invaluable.

Prioritizing relationships within OST programs is also key in supporting disabled students. Ongoing community building efforts to involve parents, promote friendship, and prevent bullying can create environments where children feel safe and experience a sense of belonging.

Evaluation Cycle

Evaluating inclusion efforts can give programs data to help identify growth, needs, and areas where professional development would be most useful. Mahoney and Haley-Mize (2017) suggests that, even though it is not focused on disability, the Youth Program Quality Assessment (YPQA) can be used as an effective program evaluation because it looks at environment and access. The Special Needs Inclusion Project (2010) also offers a thoughtful guide to monitoring an inclusive program. Thorough evaluations include feedback from families and participants, self-reflection from staff, and space to review data and set goals for improvements. Targeted professional development can help staff understand why inclusion is important and how to implement inclusive practices. Programs can evaluate, plan, monitor progress, and evaluate again, maintaining a cycle of continuous growth.

Assessments that consider access and environment tend to unearth structural issues that are usually the purview of program administrators. Lack of wheelchair accessibility in restrooms or program spaces, lack of accessible transportation or equipment, and inadequate staffing numbers are issues that usually rely on funding, but certainly need attention. Creative and collaborative solutions can emerge when these needs are made public.

Along with the evaluation of the environment and use of inclusive strategies, programs can also monitor the progress individual participants are making. Are they reaching goals? Are they participating? Dedicated time with other staff members to consider individual children is often useful for sharing and creating support strategies.

Community Outreach

Strong community outreach involves enthusiastically inviting the participation of disabled children and their families. This means providing welcoming materials with information about the access and accommodations offered by the program. When a Boys and Girls Club advertises their Include Me program on their website (Include Me, 2018), they announce to families that they see disabled children as expected participants in their club. Another positive example is a welcome message to parents. This is an example that the Union for Reform Judaism wrote for their summer camps:

> Our Inclusion Coordinators, trained professionals hired by each of our camps to support campers with special needs, are prepared to work with caregivers and professionals to plan for and provide a fulfilling camp experience for all children. Contact the Camp Director at each of our URJ Camps to discuss any accommodations or

support systems that we can put in place to ensure the success of your child. (Inclusion and Special Needs Programs, n.d.)

Websites and promotional materials can provide the first sign of a program's willingness to support disabled children and to provide information about inclusive practices used. Programs can ensure website accessibility and provide information in alternative formats. When families call or show up in person, programs have an opportunity to show their capacity for listening and working together. Open communication and collaboration with individuals, family members, and advocacy groups can greatly benefit those responsible for providing inclusive programs (Schleien et al, 2014) and the families they serve. Advocacy groups are often willing to review materials and provide feedback.

Using strengths-based language in communication can influence children and teen's desire to participate in programs. When inviting youth to become participants in an AmeriCorps mentoring program, my team and I let students know that we saw leadership potential in them. Our flyers announced a "leadership club" not an "at-risk club." Disabled youth, like their nondisabled peers, benefit from and are motivated by acknowledgement of their assets.

Provide Ongoing Professional Development

OST providers play a crucial role in disability access in programs and their lack of adequate training can create significant barriers (Mahoney & Haley-Mize, 2017). The part-time nature of many OST positions often attract young adults who are in college and retirees who may need fewer hours (Hurd & Deutsch, 2017). High turnover rates, low pay, and workers with sometimes little prior experience can make it a challenge for programs to keep well-qualified people on the job (Nee, Howe, Schmidt, & Cole, 2006).

As an inclusion specialist, I scheduled a three-day visit at a child development center and youth center to conduct observations and provide training to staff. Although I had spoken to the director on the phone, I did not mention that I am a wheelchair user. When I arrived the first day, the woman at the front desk did not welcome me when I introduced myself. She frowned and went to bring the director. The two of them stood together and whispered as they looked back at me. I finally asked if there was a problem. "This isn't gonna work," the director said. She went on to explain that their facilities were not accessible, there were steps in some classrooms.

I asked specific questions and learned the steps were all single steps. Although I wanted to leave, I pushed, "I think this can work. Are you willing to help me with the steps?" They quickly agreed and the three of us worked as a solid team during the entire visit. I found the staff to be friendly, dedicated to working well with children and families, and open to *all* of my suggestions, including the suggestion that small ramps could be added to eliminate the barrier of the steps.

In the scenario above, the staff's reaction to meeting me did not indicate their real desire to provide an inclusive environment. Rather, it points to the reality that many good providers need support in creating these environments. Not uncommon, the providers' fear of being judged as noncompliant or incapable initially appeared to be unwelcoming. When parents of disabled children arrive at the doorstep, providers are often afraid of hurting children or not being able to meet their needs (Ong, 2009). Meeting the needs of a diverse population of children and youth requires knowledge, skill, and an openness to including disabled children. A provider's attitude about inclusion certainly contributes to effective integration of disabled children (Rheams & Bain, 2005; van der Veen, Smeets, & Derriks, 2010). A survey of over 400 OST staff in New Jersey found a correlation between the level of professional development and years of experience with having positive experience with inclusion (Sharp, Rodas, & Sadovnik, 2012). While many respondents in the survey reported using resources such as parents, teachers, child study teams, health care providers, disability organizations, and the internet, those with higher numbers of years in the field were more likely to use the available resources. Many providers report a desire for more professional development, specifically in handling challenging behavior and developing inclusive programs.

Resources for supporting inclusion efforts can be found through local, state, and national organizations. A few notable sources are:

- The National AfterSchool Association, a membership organization for the profession, nurtures advocacy and development in the OST field and share resources to promote quality, inclusive programs (https://naaweb.org).
- The New York State Network for Success[4] created an online resource, Including All Children: Frequently Asked Questions about Including Students with Disabilities in Afterschool and Summer Programs (http://www.nysan.org/wp-content/uploads/2014/08/Inclusion-FAQ.pdf).
- The Special Needs Inclusion Project has created *Inclusion Tool Kit for Afterschool Programs* (http://www.snipsf.org/wp-content/uploads/2011/08/v2010Inclusion-Tool-Kit-Sept-update1.pdf).
- Kids Included Together provides a range of online and onsite training modules as well as coaching and consultation with providers (https://www.kit.org).
- Access Living provides disability peer support and advocacy in questioning stereotypes, protecting civil rights, and making social reform. (https://www.accessliving.org)

CONCLUSION: FORWARD MOTION

I want to acknowledge that no program is perfect. Even though integrated recreation programs in general have worked to provide better disability access and

---

[4] Formerly named New York State Afterschool Network.

have made marked improvements since the passage of the ADA, there is need for further work (Austin & Youngkhill, 2013; Schleien et al, 2014). Disability-specific programs also need to be vetted. Disabled individuals and their families encounter barriers to access on a daily basis and become skilled in navigating and in "choosing which battles to fight." Those who do not often face barriers to access rarely understand the energy needed to advocate. This is apparent when we mention specific problems of access. Our friends, neighbors, and colleagues offer responses like, "Did you let someone know?," "All you have to do is ask," or "Can you just call ahead and let them know what you need?"

As parents look for safety and support and consider the competition levels of activities (Mayer & Anderson, 2014), we can encourage them to also consider the messages programs give about disability and we can encourage programs to look deeply at their own intentional and unintentional messages. If our programs further stigmatize disabled children and their families, we burden them with the work of resisting or deflecting that stigma (Manago, Davis, & Goar, 2017).

I remember cringing when a friend invited me to watch her daughter play ball in the Miracle League, a community's effort to provide recreation for disabled children. What is the *miracle*? I wondered. Did someone consider it a miracle that the children could run the bases? Was it a miracle that funding came through for it? Did the name *Miracle* League make the funding possible? Despite my misgivings, I attended the game, where I had many more questions. Why did no one get *out*? Was someone afraid disabled children would not be able to handle it? How would I feel if I were a participant and people cheered for me regardless of what I did?

If we can all start considering the long-term impact of these seemingly small aspects of our programs, whether they are inclusive or disability-specific, we'll offer better programs. With intention, we must move forward without all the answers, open to learning from each other.

RESEARCH CONNECTIONS BY THE EDITORS

Suzanne Stolz raises serious and truthful questions regarding the ways that the OST field addresses (or doesn't address) the needs of disabled youth. Although the ADA law states that all programs must be inclusive, we have seen in our many years of work in the field the following to occur. Programs will not deny access to disabled youth. They will, at some point down the road after the child has been at the program for a couple of weeks, tell the parents that they do not have the resources to 'handle' the young person. And they're correct. While children and youth during the school day will have aides paid for by tax levy dollars, that doesn't extend to the afterschool or summer program. OST programs based at schools have to rely on the generosity of the principal to provide a budget for an aide to stay after hours. And that's an extremely rare occurrence. In addition, Suzanne Stolz has mentioned the correct fact that a large percentage of the workforce of the OST field are young college-aged workers. The professional development they receive often just covers the "basics" such as positive youth development and how to design a lesson or activity. There is rarely an opportunity to provide meaningful professional development in working with disabled students, or creating a welcoming and inclusive environment for disabled students.

One of the few studies of inclusion of children and youth with disabilities in OST (Galloway & Shea, 2009) found that organizations need to engage in self-assessment to determine the ways they are including and welcoming disabled youth. But that means they need to prioritize this topic out of the morass of other pressing issues, such as adequate funding and finding appropriate and affordable space to hold programs. Some of the recommendations provided by Stolz are a beginning framework for any such study, and can be easily flipped into research questions such as, "What types of language about inclusion are extant in the mission and vision of organizations?" "How are programs' inclusion philosophies implemented and translated into programs?" "What types of professional development are provided to staff on creating welcoming and inclusive programs, and how does the PD translate into program practices?" Finally, given the nature of the field, the employment of disabled folks is a critical and major question. It would be interesting to gather a national sample of staff of OST programs to determine the rate that staff with disabilities are hired. A higher number of staff with disabilities would imply that programs truly see disabled people as valuable contributors rather than recipients of services. There's still much work to be done.

REFERENCES

Annamma, S. A., Ferri, B. A., & Connor, D. J. (2018). Disability critical race theory: Exploring the intersectional lineage, emergence, and potential futures of DisCrit in education. *Review of Research in Education, 42*(1), 46–71. Retrieved from https://doi.org/10.3102/0091732X18759041

Arbour-Nicitopoulos, K. P., Grassmann, V., Orr, K., McPherson, A. C., Faulkner, G. E., & Wright, F. V. (2018). A scoping review of inclusive out-of-school time physical activity programs for children and youth with physical disabilities. *Adapted Physical Activity Quarterly, 20*(20), 1–28. doi:10.1123/apaq.2017-0012

Austin, D. R., & Youngkhill, L. (2013). *Inclusive and special recreation: Opportunities for diverse populations to flourish* (6th ed.) Champagne, IL: Sagamore Publishing.

Baglieri, S. (2012). *Disability studies and the inclusive classroom: Critical practices for creating least restrictive attitudes.* New York, NY: Routledge.

Bandy, T., & Moore, K. A. (2009). Non-participation of children and adolescents in out-of-school time programs: Child, family, and neighborhood factors. *Child Trends Publication, 39*, 1–6.

Beratan, G. D. (2008). The song remains the same: Transposition and the disproportionate representation of minority students in special education. *Race Ethnicity and Education, 11*, 337–354. doi:10.1080/13613320802478820

Brewster, S., & Coleyshaw, L. (2011). Participation or exclusion? Perspectives of pupils with autistic spectrum disorders on their participation in leisure activities. *Brit-*

ish Journal of Learning Disabilities, 39(4), 284–291. Retrieved from https://doi. org/10.1111/j.1468-3156.2010.00665.x

Charlton, J. I. (1998). *Nothing about us without us: Disability oppression and empowerment*. Oakland, CA: University of California Press.

Ferri, B. A., & Connor, D. J. (2005). Tools of exclusion: Race, disability, and (re)segregated education. *Teachers College Record, 107*, 453–474.

Galloway, F., & Shea, M. M. (2009, Fall). Does your organization welcome participants with disabilities? A New Assessment Tool. *Afterschool Matters, 9*, 13–19.

Hamilton, D. (2005). An ecobehavioural analysis of interactive engagement of children with developmental disabilities with their peers in inclusive preschools. *International Journal of Disability, Development and Education, 52*, 121–137. doi:10.1080/10349120500086363

Hayes, E., & Balcazar, F. (2008). Peer-mentoring and disability: Current applications and future directions. In T. Kroll (Ed.), *Focus on Disability: Trends in Research and Application* (pp. 89–108). Hauppauge, NY: Nova Science.

Hurd, N., & Deutsch, N. (2017). SEL-focused after-school programs. *The Future of Children, 27*(1), 95–115.

Include Me. (2018). In *Boys and girls club of tracy*. Retrieved from http://www.bgctracy. org/inclusion.php

Inclusion and Special Needs Programs. (n.d.). In *Union for Reform Judaism*. Retrieved from https://urjyouth.org/inclusion-special-needs-programs/

Information and technical assistance on the Americans with Disabilities Act. (2018). Retrieved May 25, 2018 from https://www.ada.gov/ada_title_III.htm

Kluth, P. (2010). *You're going to love this kid! Teaching students with autism in the inclusive classroom*. Baltimore, MD: Paul H Brooks.

Koster, M., Pijl, S. J., Nakken, H., & Van Houten, E. (2010). Social participation of students with special needs in regular primary education in the Netherlands. *International Journal of Disability, Development and Education, 57*, 59–75. doi:10.1080/10349120903537905

Krull, J., Wilbert, J., & Hennemann, T. (2014). The social and emotional situation of first graders with classroom behavior problems and classroom learning difficulties in inclusive classes. *Learning Disabilities–A Contemporary Journal, 12*, 161–190.

Lalvani P., & Polvere L. (2013). Historical perspectives on studying families of children with disabilities: A case for critical research. *Disability Studies Quarterly, 33*, 3.

Lindsay, S., McPherson, A. C., Aslam, H., McKeever, P., & Wright, V. (2012). Exploring children's perceptions of two school-based social inclusion programs: A pilot study. *Child & Youth Care Forum, 42*:1–18. doi:10.1007/s10566-012-9183-9

Magill-Evans, J., Darrah, J., & Adkins, R. (2003). Youths with cerebral palsy and their satisfaction with recreational services: implications for inclusion. *Leisure/Loisir, 28*(1–2), 71–86.

Mahoney, J. L., & Haley-Mize, S. (2017). Knowing better, doing better: Three gaps to fill in the next decade of research in out-of-school time. In H. J. Malone & T. Donahue (Eds.), *The growing out-of-school time field: Past, present, and future* (pp. 267–292). Charlotte, NC: Information Age Publishing.

Manago, B., Davis, J. L., & Goar, C. (2017). Discourse in action: Parents' use of medical and social models to resist disability stigma. *Social Science & Medicine, 184*, 169–177.

Mayer, W. E., & Anderson, L. S. (2014). Perceptions of people with disabilities and their families about segregated and inclusive recreation involvement. *Therapeutic Recreation Journal, 48*(2), 150.

Mobily, K. E., & Dieser, R. B. (2018). Seeking alternatives in therapeutic recreation/recreation therapy: a social/recreation community model. *Leisure/Loisir, 42*(1), 1–23.

Morris, R. P., Fletcher-Smith, J. C., & Radford, K. A. (2017). A systematic review of peer mentoring interventions for people with traumatic brain injury. *Clinical Rehabilitation, 31*(8), 1030–1038.

Mullins, C. K. (2015). *A phenomenological study of participation in specialized and inclusive recreation programs.* Online Theses and Dissertations, 407. Retrieved from https://encompass.eku.edu/etd/407

Nee, J., Howe, P., Schmidt, C., & Cole, P. (2006). *Understanding the after-school workforce: Opportunities and challenges for an emerging profession.* Charlestown, MA: National Afterschool Association.

Nondiscrimination on the basis of disability by public accommodations and in commercial facilities. (1991). *28 C.F.R. § 36* Retrieved from https://www.ecfr.gov/cgi-bin/text-idx?c=ecfr&SID=2ab2aab2d3d2fd0f544a5ce7aad8f04c&rgn=div5&view=text&node=28:1.0.1.1.37&idno=28#_top

Odom, S., Buysee, V., & Soukakou, E. (2011). Inclusion for young children with disabilities: A quarter century of research perspectives. *Journal of Early Intervention, 33*(4), 344–356. doi:

Ong, F. (Ed.). (2009). *Inclusion works! Creating child care programs that promote belonging for children with special needs.* Children Development Division, California Department of Education. Retrieved from https://www.cde.ca.gov/sp/cd/re/documents/inclusionworks.pdf

Pearson, K. (2018). *Response to drive-by lawsuits.* Retrieved from https://equalrightscenter.org/response-drive-lawsuits/

Piškur, B., Meuser, S., Jongmans, M. J., Ketelaar, M., Smeets, R. J., Casparie, B. M., Haarsma, F. A., & Beurskens, A. J. (2016). The lived experience of parents enabling participation of their child with a physical disability at home, at school and in the community. *Disability and Rehabilitation, 38*(8), 803–812.

Rheams, T. A., & Bain, S. K. (2005). Social interaction interventions in an inclusive era: attitudes of teachers in early childhood self-contained and inclusive settings. *Psychology in the Schools, 42*, 53–63. doi:10.1002/pits.20029.

Rhodes, J. E., & DuBois, D. L. (2008). Mentoring relationships and programs for youth. *Current Directions in Psychological Science, 17*(4), 254–258.

Ruijs, N. M., Van der Veen, I., & Peetsma, T. D. (2010). Inclusive education and students without special educational needs. *Educational Research, 52*(4), 351–390.

Sapon-Shevin, M. (2010). *Because we can change the world: A practical guide to building cooperative, inclusive classroom communities.* Thousand Oaks, CA: Corwin Press.

Schleien, S. J., Miller, K. D., Walton, G., & Pruett, S. (2014). Parent perspectives of barriers to child participation in recreational activities. *Therapeutic Recreation Journal, 48*(1), 61.

Sharp, J., Rodas, E. R., & Sadovnik, A. R. (2012). Supporting youth with special needs in out-of-school time: A study of OST providers in New Jersey. *Afterschool Matters, 16*, 31–41.

Solis, S. (2006). I'm "coming out" as disabled, but I'm "staying in" to rest: Reflecting on elected and imposed segregation. *Equity & Excellence in Education, 39*(2), 146–153.

Special Needs Inclusion Project. (2010). *Inclusion Toolkit.* Retrieved from http://www.snipsf.org/wp-content/uploads/2011/08/v2010Inclusion-Tool-Kit-Sept-update1.pdf

Stolz, S. (2016). Disability community, policy, care and empowerment: "Growing up" at MDA camp and the shaky social contract. In R. Malhotra (Ed.) *Disability politics in a global economy: Essays in honour of marta russell* (pp. 166–180). New York, NY: Routledge.

Stumbo, N. J., Wang, Y., & Pegg, S. (2011). Issues of access: What matters to people with disabilities as they seek leisure experiences. *World Leisure Journal, 53*(2), 91–103.

Symes, W., & Humphrey, N. (2010). Peer-group indicators of social inclusion among pupils with autistic spectrum disorders (ASD) in mainstream secondary schools: A comparative study. *School Psychology International, 31,* 478–494. doi:10.1177/0143034310382496.

Taylor, M., & Houghton, S. (2008). Difficulties in initiating and sustaining peer friendships: Perspectives on students diagnosed with AD/HD. *British Journal of Special Education, 35,* 209–219.

Thompson, D., & Emira, M. (2011). "They say every child matters, but they don't:" An investigation into parental and career perceptions of access to leisure facilities and respite care for children and young people with autism spectrum disorder (ASD) or attention deficit, hyperactivity disorder (ADHD). *Disability & Society, 26*(1), 65–78. doi: 10.1080/09687599.2011.529667

Wiart, L., Darrah, J., Kelly, M., & Legg, D. (2015). Community fitness programs: What is available for children and youth with motor disabilities and what do parents want? *Physical & Occupational Therapy in Pediatrics, 35*(1), 73–87.

van der Veen I, Smeets E, & Derriks M. (2010). Children with special educational needs in the Netherlands: number, characteristics and school career. *Educational Research, 52,* 15–43.

PART III

EQUITY THROUGH CRITICAL PRACTICE

CHAPTER 6

CRITICAL YOUTH DEVELOPMENT

Living and Learning at the Intersections of Life

Merle McGee

" James!" I startled the 16 year old standing near me on the subway platform. "Oh hey miss," he said with a slight smile. It was 2:00 am on a Tuesday night in New York City, and we both knew in a few hours we would see one another in class. I walked away from my friend on the platform to investigate the intentions of this young man I had grown to know over the previous six months. James' family had emigrated from the Caribbean for a 'better life,' but he had recently made some poor choices that landed him before a juvenile court judge. The judge sentenced James to the alternative-to-incarceration program where I worked in the education unit. James struck me as thoughtful, critical of the world around him, and more capable than his school performance to date would reveal. James was also a young father and talked about 'doing better' for his baby. "Where you headed?" I asked. He flashed a knowing smile. "Why are you out here?" I continued, "Man, you know nothing good can come from being in the streets at this hour." I reminded him about our conversations regarding his choices and that the program offered him a reset button. He nodded his head in obligatory agreement. As the train pulled into the station I shouted, "Don't be late tomorrow, and if you are, remember I know why." Within

Changemakers! Practitioners Advance Equity and Access in Out-of-School Time Programs,
pages 93–108.
Copyright © 2019 by Information Age Publishing
All rights of reproduction in any form reserved.

two months of our subway encounter James would be gunned down by the police in the early morning hours on a city street. He would be the fourth person killed by police in that month. It would be nearly ten years before I fully understood why I had misdirected my anger over his death at him instead of the institutions that weave a web of dispossession.

This experience as a young youth worker disrupted my narrative of hope and shook me to the core. I had entered the youth development field believing that every problem could be solved with copious amounts of hope and enthusiasm. Instead, the real world has disrupted that narrative time and again and revealed the harsh realities young people face and the environments in which they face obstacles. I was angry, heartbroken, and lamenting the loss of a potential unfulfilled.

Years later, as a seasoned youth worker, I mourned the death of Tamir Rice and Rekia Boyd at the hands of police. As with James, I was left to make sense of the circumstances that created these tragedies and came to realize these incidents were symptomatic of structural racism, that is, racism embedded in and reinforced by many of our institutions including schools, law enforcement, and media (Fulbright-Anderson, Lawrence, Sutton, Susi, & Kubisch, 2005). I have also come to realize that my understanding of these and many other incidents emerged because of a lifelong journey to explore my race and gender identity and the sociological structures that impact people of color and whites as well. In this chapter I delve into the principles, theoretical frames, and strategies that can explore and address these phenomena. I am defining this approach as Critical Youth Development (CYD), which will be described in the next section. It is my belief that this approach to working with youth can be used to understand and, to some degree, mitigate the impact of how social institutions negatively impact youth.

YOUTH DEVELOPMENT & THE ROOTS
OF CRITICAL YOUTH DEVELOPMENT

Traditional youth development frameworks focus on youth as assets to the community, building upon or adding to young people's social, ethical, emotional, physical, creative, and cognitive competencies (Guerra & Bradshaw, 2008). Practitioners using these frameworks have offered important approaches to building life skills, personal agency, and resiliency to reduce risky behaviors and promote youth's vision for the future. Youth development frameworks also include gender and culturally responsive approaches to working with youth that recognize the importance of intersecting identities and cultural humility practices, which offer practitioners an opportunity to engage youth as co-constructors of knowledge and to structure effective activities and meaningful programs.

Youth, as well as youth workers, operate in a world where racialized trauma enacted by policing, criminal justice, gender inequities, and institutions such as schools uniquely impact lived experiences and life options. During my tenure at a college prep program in New York City, my colleagues Maurice Mangwiro and Drs. Deidre Franklin, Bianca Baldridge, and Nancy Cha and I recognized that tackling internalized and interpersonal racism alone would not fully equip our youth to understand the barriers as well as privileges of living under white supremacy and a legacy of colonialism. We realized that discussing race explicitly and its meaning in personal development helped youth more fully understand their identities and how their identities are shaped by the broader historical context and social narrative. However, it became imperative to us that youth at our program understood the broader institutional and structural manifestations of a social arrangement that left them experiencing an imbalance of power, privilege, and oppression.

My colleagues and I believed that for both youth at the margins and those with social and cultural privilege, the ability to navigate discussions around identity, power, privilege, and oppression and to leverage these explorations to advance social justice was an important life skill. I contend, and will demonstrate in this chapter, that youth development practitioners can create a space in which youth can explore and develop through critical youth development (CYD).

MY PRESENCE IS NOT AN APOLOGY: APPLYING CYD TO FIRST GENERATION COLLEGE STUDENTS OF COLOR

For many years I worked with high potential college-bound youth in New York City. I came to this work because I had benefited from caring adults that nurtured my college aspirations. I had found in my community a network of parents, educators, and aunties that provided financial support, words of encouragement, and tough love when I wanted to give up. Perhaps most meaningful were the talks with my grandmother. She had fought for local school integration and lamented as she listened to my frustrations with navigating the racial dynamics of my predominantly white college. She and I wondered how I could survive the daily racial microaggressions[1] (Sue et al., 2007) that hindered my comfort, emotional wellbeing, and ultimately my learning. Years later, I chose to repay her support by becoming a youth development practitioner, convinced I could share with others the care and support she offered and which I credit for my own ability to persist in college and life.

I devoted myself to a program located in a Central Harlem neighborhood that was in transition after years of neglect and underinvestment. The neighborhood was undergoing a renaissance that included an explosion of housing investments, business development, and the beginnings of the charter school movement. There were a limited number of schools in the area that met the academic standards set by state education guidelines and the organization responded to parents' dissatisfaction with local schools. Our students were high potential youth who needed support. The organization experienced success in helping these youth prepare for

---

[1] Racial Microaggressions are commonplace verbal or behavioral indignities, whether intentional or unintentional, which communicate hostile, derogatory, or negative racial slights and insults.

and gain access to competitive institutions. The program supported collegiate aspirations through academic and social and emotional preparedness.

We kept in touch with our students, and unfortunately, heard about how their excitement and pride of attending college gave way to feeling emotionally drained by navigating subtle to overt interpersonal and institutional racism. Students shared stories of a dorm mate's inquiries about their presumed criminality or that of their family members. Young people were approached by campus security telling them not to gather or checking their identification cards. Students reported that professors routinely validated racialized commentary and invalidated their lived experiences as a part of class discourse. The racial microaggressions from peers, faculty, and campus security were compounded by the inadequate response or lack of institutional support from residential assistants and administrators and resulted in hostile classrooms, dorm rooms, and campus life. Countless students reached out to us for support and validation or sought to return to the familiarity of their local communities. Students reported feeling socially isolated and ill-equipped to process their experiences of institutional bias.

Our youth's experiences gave birth to CYD and continues to demonstrate the relevance and applicability of this framework. My colleagues and I turned our attention to models that would support young people's understanding of self within the context of institutions and directly confront racial and class realities they experienced at school and on the streets of New York City. We began to extend the framework to include an examination of how institutions validated gender, race, and other identities. Youth needed to understand how power, privilege, and oppression within predominantly white institutions functioned. Through the CYD framework, youth examine feelings regarding their identity and the social landscape they inhabit. During dialogue youth can experience and exercise curiosity and care for others while fostering interconnectedness, interdependence, and cross-racial/cultural learning. Mapping one's identity helped students understand how classroom microaggressions were fundamental to reinforcing dominant cultural norms and that they should not expect to be rescued from them but learn how to hold agents with power accountable within the institution.

CRITICAL YOUTH DEVELOPMENT PRACTICE

Critical Youth Development (CYD) is designed to critique and disrupt the dominant social narratives about race, gender and class, and reimagine a more inclusive and equitable future for youth. CYD is rooted in critical pedagogy[2] (Freire, 1968) and draws from critical race theory[3] (Bell, 1973; Delgado & Stefancic,

---

[2] Critical Pedagogy applies a critical analysis to education and learning as a tool for examining social justice issues.

[3] Critical Race Theory is an analytical framework used to examine how racialized power and privilege create power structures which benefit white people and marginalize people of color.

1993; Ladson-Billings & Tate, 1995), and identity development (Cross, 1971; Helms, 1993) at the intersections of power, privilege, and oppression.

CYD involves a structural analysis of social identities and social systems that keep all intersecting oppressions in place (Crenshaw, 1991). CYD recognizes the importance of naming racialized and gender-based trauma, and the intersecting experiences of identities (e.g. race, class, and gender). My colleagues and I designed the approach to be used in multiracial/multicultural settings to engender learning, interconnectedness, interdependence, and solidarity across groups.

Key Components

There are several key principles that are important to understanding and implementing CYD. First, CYD addresses youth's institutional and structural ecosystem; it conceptualizes an understanding of power, privilege and oppression as a leadership competency; and it teaches youth how to harness a diversity of perspectives to enhance cooperation and innovation. There are several core components in our approach to implementing CYD. They include:

- An explicit analysis of power, privilege, and oppression;
- Experiential activities that foster self-awareness and reflection for both youth and youth practitioners;
- Incubators to build trust and support growth;
- Alternative approaches to cultivating leadership practices.

Brave Spaces-Embracing Discomfort. To enable meaningful exploration, youth practitioners must create a space where youth can feel vulnerable and grapple with personal experiences related to power, privilege, and oppression. We have found that creating a brave space (Arao & Clemens, 2013) is conducive to achieving the vulnerable stance required to forge new learning. Unlike a "safe space" used in much of the programmatic language and literature in youth development, which conflates safety with comfort, a brave space helps youth, as well as staff, lean into discomfort as a necessary condition for growth.

Brave spaces foster mutual respect, promote psychological and emotional wellbeing and dispel the myth that one can remain in their comfort zone and still learn new ways of thinking and being. The very nature of learning requires bravery because "learning necessarily involves not merely risk, but pain of giving up a former condition in favor of a new way of seeing things" (Boomstrom, 1998, p. 399). In order to ask youth to stretch or change and accept discomfort or maybe even emotional pain, we must reassure them that the experience is one they can survive and from which they can benefit by creating an incubator for self-discovery.

I have found it necessary within a brave space to articulate grounding principles to make sure that dialogue can occur. Examples of grounding principles include a) making connection, b) building community and c) engaging in reflection.

The principles are flexible, can be co-constructed with young people, and can reflect an organization's values. Once developed, practitioners should spend time unpacking their grounding principles to achieve a shared understanding so that they, in turn, can help their group create agreements and put them into operation. These agreements are especially important because disagreements and discomfort will emerge during CYD.

Avoiding Request for Comfort Agreements. There are three proposed agreements that often come up during a discussion about group agreements which present a challenge to dialogues about power, privilege, and oppression. They include: assume the best intentions, do not take anything personally, and agree to disagree. I call these "request for comfort" agreements. In a culturally neutral context these ground rules are viewed as innocuous. However, within a framework of power, privilege, and oppression, these agreements can be experienced as emotional weapons that trigger and traumatize marginalized individuals, while likely preserving the comfort of dominant participants, silencing marginalized participants, and negatively impacting the emotional well-being of groups most affected by oppression. The "request for comfort" agreements not only derail dialogue and learning but can also reinforce systems of oppression within the brave spaces CYD practitioners seek to create.

Assume the best intentions can be a risky position for historically marginalized groups. The expectation of trust without earning it, especially in cross-racial dialogues, reinforces the privilege of members who hold more power—including the adults in the room. An alternate agreement could include "assume positive intentions AND acknowledge impact." *Do not take anything personally* is a potentially emotionally unsafe request based on a group member's experience with oppressive people or institutions. This agreement can also allow those causing harm to avoid owning the impact of their words or behavior. Even though one doesn't mean to harm another, the harmed party is still left to deal with the results. An alternate agreement could include "honor lived experiences" to make clear that what is privileged learning for one person may be painful personal experience for another. Lastly, *agree to disagree* is a convenient tool that allows groups to avoid learning. It assumes that all viewpoints are equally valid and fails to articulate an analysis of power and privilege as well as what is oppressive and what is not.

Creating the necessary conditions for a brave space asks practitioners to recognize and resist oppressive behaviors, to examine and name our pockets of dominance and subordination vis-a-vis others, and to focus on those most impacted by oppression so that the process of dialogue is itself anti-oppressive.

Identity and Institutions—The Right to Define. CYD explores social identity development because young people, as members of society, are subject to its rules regarding socially constructed identities and their meaning. Given youths' compulsory interactions with institutions, it is vital that youth practitioners examine the ways institutions shape both their own and youths' internal perceptions and external realities. CYD invites youth to unpack identities, both how they see themselves and how others perceive them.

To explore youths' personal ecosystem, tools must be provided to help them examine social hierarchies such as race, class, gender, sexual orientation, and religion. Some ways that CYD facilitators can do so is by guiding youth via asset mapping activities, journaling, or cross-cultural dialogues to foster analytical thinking and self-reflection. A thorough exploration of how identities are constructed and lived within our society helps youth make sense of both the opportunities available to them and the challenges they face.

CYD exploration begins by creating groups of young people generally by identities that are most meaningful to them. (Note: Gender specific cohorts have been used, but careful consideration should be exercised to ensure trans and gender-nonconforming youth inclusion as well). These groups help youth understand how various identities are constructed and animated. Youth learn and define key terms for complex social phenomena like race, gender, and class. Experiential activities help expose youth to factors that form a person's identity and how they are socialized early in life into their identities.

Human beings receive messages about gender usually from birth. As CYD facilitators, we engage youth in dialogue to examine uncontested ideas about what girls and boys can and cannot do, the primacy of a gender binary and invite youth to consider gender differences. In the case of gender, youth often notice and identify gender inequities within their own family. Facilitators interrogate language that is used to signal identity expectations within family and among peers. Statements such as 'man up' or 'act like a lady' are critiqued for bias. These dialogues help students recognize pockets of power and oppression within their lives, particularly for those whose gender identity or expression challenges societal norms. The following are some activities that we used to help youth explore and challenge societal norms.

Activity #1: Pieces of a Pie

"Pieces of a Pie" is an activity we have used to highlight power dynamics within identity exploration. This activity is a power, privilege, and oppression self-inventory and should be done only after the group has formed a bond and feels comfortable being vulnerable with each other. Each member is given a 'pie pan' and individual 'slices' of two colors. Unknown to the participants, the colors represent pockets of privilege or oppression. The facilitator explains that as each statement is read, if it is true to an individual, the participant then select the corresponding colored slice. Statements include:

> I am a male/female, I am straight/LGBTQ, I am White/Person of Color, My family owns their home, I don't hesitate to use public restroom that matches my gender, I have a disability/No disability, Most of my teachers look like me, I can hold hands with my partner without fear of harassment, My religious holidays are recognized

by my school, I can expect to see myself on TV, and People assume I deserve to be in a honors course.

Once the list of items is read, participants are asked to place the pieces in a pie and to count the number of each color they possess. Once complete, the facilitator explains that each color represents the amount of privilege or oppression your identity provides you within our society. It is usually shocking to observe how much privilege a person possesses or oppression they may experience. On the other hand, an individual might have an abundance of oppression, and still have privilege relative to others.

This exercise is followed by a robust dialogue to unpack content, learning and emotions related to each statement and the activity. To observe a 'pie' filled with aspects of who you are as a person and how you are perceived within a larger social context can be emotional, yet necessary for participants to develop the empathy required to explore their identity and that of others. Most people do not consciously live their lives as 'oppressed' people or as an oppressor, but this exercise brings forth awareness and with it important questions.

Activity #2: Neighborhood Walk. The media is an institution that looms large in a young person's social ecosystem. Many young people are consumers of media and some are co-creators of media through social media. CYD facilitators engage youth in an analysis of media, how is it constructed and for whom. Young people learn that media is not neutral, and messages are created with a point of view. Youth practice deciphering media perspectives by noting the language and images used to convey a message.

A popular and enlightening activity is a neighborhood walk through an historically under-resourced neighborhood followed by a walk through an over-resourced community. Youth walk the neighborhood and act as researchers, recording the number and types of advertisements. They note who are in the ads, what is being advertised, and the target audience(s). Once the data collection is complete, facilitators engage youth in a discussion. Almost universally, youth notice an over-saturation of particular types of ads in poorer communities, such as those for alcohol. Conversely, youth note the minimal presence of this advertising in wealthier communities, and, when present, it is focused on luxury products. Naturally, this exploration creates an opportunity to reflect on how class and race intersect and are reinforced by the media.

Leadership Competencies—Harnessing the Power of Diversity. As a nation, we struggle to truthfully educate our youth about structural inequities rooted in race and gender, and thereby impede their ability to transform these same inequities. CYD amplifies the relevance of identity awareness, institutional impact, and power and privilege not only for youth development, but also for youth leadership. Young people learn that leadership is not simply bestowed but exercised through actions. CYD differs in its approach to leadership from other youth leadership approaches in that advancing equity is central to the very definition of leadership. Our work with young people is to help them develop anti-oppressive leadership styles that foster more accountability in cross racial/cultural and gendered interactions.

Youth are invited to observe ways in which power is used and how it is necessary to confront internal, interpersonal, and institutional bias. Over the years of my practice, whenever I encountered a superhero masquerading as an unruly youth, I would wonder with them "What if you used your leader powers for good instead of evil?" I would often be met with inquisitive looks, but it was enough to distract from the undesired behavior long enough to share power as opposed to struggle over it. My approach to power dynamics utilizes a power framework that identifies distinct expressions. These forms of expression are a) *power over;* b) *power within; c) power to; and d) power with* (VeneKlasen, Miller, Budlender, & Clark, 2002).

Power over is traditionally how we think about power as the ability to get someone to do something by using rewards, punishment, and manipulation. *Power within* signifies self-esteem, confidence that comes from gaining self-awareness, and realizing the possibility of acting. *Power to* describes acting once an individual learns it is possible to act. *Power with* embraces the ability to influence and act based on cooperation and being in solidarity with others.

Exploring these expressions of power with young people helps them understand, critique, and subvert oppressive social phenomenon such as racism and misogyny, and understand how power operates at the macro (institutional/structural) and micro (interpersonal, internalized) levels. It emphasizes the importance of personal agency and interpersonal cooperation to challenge unhealthy social norms.

Activity #3: Building a Home. Power is hard to explain to young people because it is often invisible and difficult to deconstruct due to its intersecting and complex formation. Young people, however, can learn to identify and articulate how power operates in their lives through experiential activities. One which my colleagues and I have used to highlight social control is called "building a home." Students are divided into unequal size groups and placed in separate areas of a room. Students are unaware of the social status assigned to their group. The smallest group represents the upper-class group and has no more than three people. The second largest group represents the middle class and has five to seven members. The largest group represents the lowest class and consists of eight or more members.

Each group receives a set of resources to build a home within an allotted amount of time, usually 20 minutes. The upper-class group receives a prefabricated paper home and a set of images of luxury items to enhance their house. This may include images of cars, boats, pets, pools and landscaping. Additionally, they are given more supplies, such as tape, glue, scissors, relative to the size of the group. The middle-class group receives a variety of sturdy building materials and ample supplies. This group's building materials are enhanced with a few luxury items like a car and a pet. Finally, the lower-class group is given two brown sandwich bags, a marker, popsicle stick, and virtually no other supplies with which to build their home.

As the facilitators observe each group's work, they offer feedback to group members about their efforts. The upper-class group is praised for the beauty of the home and offered help by facilitators to complete the task. The middle-class group is complimented on their ingenuity and cooperation with one another to complete the task. Facilitators also offer the group advice on how to complete the task. The lower-class group doesn't receive praise or compliments about their work or offers of additional services. Facilitators even plant doubts about the quality and beauty of their homes.

As the activity progresses, we have noticed the middle-class group develop effective teamwork strategies to complete the task. The upper-class group leisurely enjoys the labor and support of the facilitators. Finally, the lower-class group begins to fray under the frustration of too many people, and not enough resources. Squabbles emerge about the best building approach once the facilitators have planted doubts in group members' minds. Once time is up, the groups present their homes and it begins to dawn on each group the privileges they were provided and how the facilitators wielded power to uplift or denigrate the group. Intensely and tangibly, students understand the expressions of power within the group's dynamic and the face of power as exercised by the facilitators. This exercise is then debriefed with youth to highlight how social class is used to bestow power or oppress groups. The invitation to youth is to resist replicating oppressive leader behaviors by first developing self-awareness and then actively reflecting on their impact on others that is rooted in shared liberation.

Doing the Work—Staff Preparation & Social Identity

"So Jorge," I said, "how would you racially describe yourself?" "I am Dominican," He replied. I probe, "Yes, I get that is your nationality or ethnicity, but racially how do you identify?" Now looking confused, Jorge replied again, "I'm Spanish then." Jorge was brown skinned and possessed a phenotype typical of a person from the African diaspora. Moreover, his mother's complexion was an even richer brown, and she had tightly coiled hair. With this knowledge, I stated "How can that be Jorge, your mother is a black woman?" He shot me an incredulous look and matter-of-factly stated, "My mother is not black," I was confused. He continued, "There are no black people in the Dominican Republic." My confusion turned to bewilderment and frustration.

Was I wrong in my racial assessment? How could he not see the obvious? Was I wrong to offer my assessment? What did I miss? I know now that what I missed was the responsibility, as a facilitator, to understand how our identities are shaped not only by family, friends, and community, but also by institutions and power structures signaling who is worthy. I learned that history, cultural norms, and attitudes about various social identities and their meaning vary among different cultural groups who may seemingly share a common diaspora. I was struck by how the U.S. context of race has been codified in specific ways that appear less obvious in other global contexts even if they are no less experienced as significant barriers to social inclusion or impediments to success. It is necessary to stretch beyond a U.S. context to understand how bicultural youth construct their identities and how they differ from youth experiencing multiple generations in the U.S. Most importantly, I needed to do my own social identity work first.

It is imperative that youth development practitioners are well versed in the historical context within which they are engaging youth. Youth practitioners must first grapple with understanding their own identities through discussion, self-reflection, reading, and exploratory activities such as journaling and other exercises to create the same intellectual and emotional responses we are likely to see in our youth. My colleagues and I jokingly refer to excavating power, privilege, and oppression within our own social identities as 'doing the work.' The work of self-exploration is never ending and at times, quite painful.

My Own Social Identity. I grew up in a racially mixed suburban town exposed to adult role models and teachers who reflected my racial and gender identity. I fondly recall the uplifting messages I received about my race from my grandparents and parents who had lived through Jim Crow, segregation, and the civil rights era, and who served as living historical memorials of racial progress made over their lifetime. The nation had moved towards a colorblind narrative that firmly rooted itself in a meritocracy. Both my home and school reinforced the personal responsibility narrative and its tenets of hard work and individual achievement. I moved through the world comfortable in my skin and confident in my intellect until I ran into the crushing reality of institutional racism embodied in my 3rd grade teacher. Ms. Sebring would have a lasting impact on my self-esteem and assessment of my capabilities. She was a white southern woman who brought with her many of the attitudes and beliefs of her ilk who were barely a decade beyond so-called desegregation in the southern United States.

My school year with Ms. Sebring was fraught with conflict over her frequent denigrating microaggressions and racialized slights that left me marked as a "troublemaker." Her microaggressions became assaults when she declared to the class that a reading group comprised of mostly students of color were "stupid monkeys." Even at 8 years old, I understood that she crossed a racial line and I challenged her doing so. I was promptly sent to the principal's office and reprimanded for talking back to a teacher whether they were right or wrong. The principal, a black man, continued his admonishment until my father arrived. After their private exchange of words my father and I headed home for the day. I was suspended for the offense.

I learned that day, as a black girl, that defense of my personhood would be met with little regard and likely with punishment. I also learned that people with individual bias and authority could employ the power of institutions to shape my life experiences. At a young age I intuitively understood interpersonal and institutional racism. I also began to understand how someone is socialized into their identity, and this socialization informs how we engage with the world. Most importantly, I realized that years of internalizing negative narratives of one's social inferiority can impact you the rest of your life.

It's painful to reflect on these incidents, but necessary to cultivate the empathy required when facilitating these types of dialogue. Having a grasp on our own socialization and a thoughtful analysis of our own beliefs and attitudes allows us to explore more deeply with our youth. Youth practitioners can gain from professional development to help them explore racial identity development, implicit bias, stereotype threat[4] and other related theories, to develop facilitation and process skills to help youth make meaning from their own experiences. These skills include creating brave space agreements, selecting and structuring appropriate exercises, honing active listening skills, balancing inquiry and advocacy when exploring a contentious topic and, finally, empathy. Practitioners' training and skill building can also be accompanied with personal practices such as counseling, healing circles, dialogue groups, and effective supervision.

ACKNOWLEDGING AND HEALING
TRAUMA—JOY THROUGH TEARS

As youth practitioners we must acknowledge and be prepared to respond to the trauma that youth experience in their schools, communities, and even their homes. Our youth inherit both generational and personal trauma as a result of interactions with biased institutions. CYD works to name and disrupt the systemic inequities that result from trauma.

I shared the following thoughts with the young people I worked with when Trayvon Martin was murdered in 2012. *"I wanted to offer encouraging words that would transcend the ugly truth of the moment. I had hoped by now I could make sense of it all. Find hope in this tragedy to alleviate your cynicism about the way things are. But the truth is, I too struggle to separate the shadow of history from the progress of today."*

My willingness to name and explore my emotional response to this incident signaled to youth that trauma was real, and that naming and reflecting on trauma would be a necessary step towards healing. Trayvon's death brought to the surface a memory I had from when, as a child of nine, my neighbor was gunned down by the police when he panicked and ran away from an officer while walking through a so-called bad neighborhood at the wrong time. This memory still shapes my attitudes about the potential of death when encountering police and bears the footprint of trauma.

The interactions of youth in marginalized communities with biased institutions, from education and healthcare to law enforcement and criminal justice, and the internalized oppression they manifest, create an unending cycle of trauma.

---

[4] Stereotype threat is a predicament in which people are or feel themselves to be at risk of conforming to stereotypes about their social group.

The constant exposure to images of unarmed black people being killed by police, undocumented family members being ripped from loved ones, detained and then deported as well as the heightened hateful rhetoric of the 2016 election cycle, trauma at the hands of structural inequities seems even more pervasive than ever. Some youth suffer from complex post-traumatic stress disorder (Perry & Szalavitz, 2006), a theory that captures the complexity of recurring traumatic stress that urban youth experience due to prolonged exposure to community and state sponsored violence. State sponsored violence can take the form of police brutality, mass incarceration, school pushout, the school to prison pipeline, mass detention, deportation, homelessness or stress caused by racism, misogyny, transphobia, and xenophobia.

Trauma-Informed Care

Trauma-informed care has emerged as an important response to the neurological, biological, psychological, and social effects of youth's interactions with biased institutions. A trauma informed approach, which complements, rather than replaces CYD, is vital in understanding how cultural racism negatively impact youth's abilities to build authentic knowledge of self and relationships beyond their own cultural groups. The generational effects of racialized trauma inhibits empathy and dehumanizes everyone in a structurally oppressive society.

According to the Substance Abuse and Mental Health Services Administration, a branch of the U.S. Health and Human Services, practitioners of the methodology must realize the widespread impact of trauma and understand potential paths for recovery; recognize the signs and symptoms of trauma in clients, families, staff, and others involved with the system; respond by fully integrating knowledge about trauma into policies, procedures, and practices; and seek to actively resist re-traumatization.

Trauma-informed care offers a useful framework to begin to understand the effects of trauma on youth and self. Youth practitioners would do well to engage experts in this approach to train staff, provide technical support, and provide capacity building activities to implement trauma informed care with a lens that addresses the unique vulnerabilities of girls of color, immigrants of color, LBGTQ and gender nonconforming youth. Youth practitioners must recognize the compounded effect of harm experienced by youth when they hold multiple marginalized identities that form their experiences. It is also important to examine whether an organization's practices and policies mitigate or reinforce trauma for participants and staff alike.

The emotional labor required to witness and attend to trauma also necessitates that youth practitioners, particularly in community-based organizations, develop self-care and healing practices and teach them to youth as well. These include physical, spiritual, emotional, creative, and community practices such as meditation, music, cyphers (a cultural practice with roots in West African traditions in which artists collaborate on music, spoken word, dance or rap), gathering with friends, and recapturing lost collective cultural practices. These types of activities provide an outlet to recuperate, recover, and find joy to fuel a person's engagement in work and life and offers a sustainable alternative to burn out. "Doing the work" requires a commitment to self-reflection, lifelong learning, healing practices, and cultural humility to create inclusive community dialogue.

CONCLUSION

In this chapter, I argue that Critical Youth Development is rooted in three core practices; first, youth development practice should include an explicit exploration of social identity development with young people on an intrapersonal and structural level; next, youth development practitioners must cultivate a nurturing, supportive and brave space to ensure young's people self-exploration is rooted in an equity framework; and finally to successfully implement a critical youth development approach, each youth practitioner must engage in their own cultural, social and identity exploration to effectively engage youth in a journey of self-discovery. With an understanding of the power analysis of society, self-awareness and humility, youth can see how to develop personal agency, work across boundaries of difference to challenge social norms, and transform institutions to make them more equitable and inclusive.

Our youth should not be left on their own to decipher structural racism and oppression. It is only by making explicit their impact on youth development, and intentionally intervening through an expanded Critical Youth Development frame, that we can begin to chart a different path for our children.

RESEARCH CONNECTIONS FROM THE EDITORS

The advancement of CYD is reminiscent of when positive youth development (PYD) was first conceptualized. At the time PYD stood in stark contrast to the deficit and pathological model of working with young people. CYD pushes against the dominant gender, race, and sexual norms at a time when marginalized communities are rapidly growing and incidents of privilege and oppression are increasingly visible on social media and in the news.

Merle McGee points out that CYD requires staff and youth have parallel journeys. Staff must "do the work" so that youth can address power, privilege, and oppression. What do these journeys entail? The youth development field would greatly benefit from case studies chronicling the parallel journeys of staff and youth. While each journey is personal and unique, case studies can illustrate the multiple avenues to growth, the ways that staff and youths' journeys intersect, and how both staff and youth navigate the inevitable setbacks.

Merle McGee asserts that professional development is essential for staff to effectively use CYD. Not only does the CYD framework require staff to introduce complex concepts and facilitate nuanced discussions, it also causes staff to modify widespread understandings of high-quality practices. For example, creating a safe and supportive environment is commonly accepted as inherent to high quality programs, yet Merle McGee demonstrates how this practice interferes with CYD and the ability of youth to develop a critical lens. To better understand this transition, and in some cases, transformation, we need to study some of the following questions: "What kinds of issues do staff encounter when facilitating CYD?" "How do staff manage these issues to preserve young people's growth?" Larson and Walker's studies of dilemmas in youth work present a clear example of how research can be used to surface dilemmas specific to facilitating CYD.

The CYD framework is a powerful tool that can be used to shift the mindsets of youth and adults. Research should explore the resulting changes in dispositions, actions, and perspectives. For example, conventional notions of developing leadership skills in young people, unlike CYD, rarely encompass how to help youth advance equity in their spheres of influence. What kinds of leadership do we see from youth who have been exposed to CYD? We may also ask, how do young people's understanding of their own identities evolve once youth become more attuned to the forces of power, privilege, and oppression? These questions, and others that focus on how youth benefit from CYD, will enhance our understanding of personal growth and identity development.

REFERENCES

Arao, B., & Clemens, K. (2013). From safe spaces to brave spaces: A new way to frame dialogue around diversity and social justice. In L. Landreman (Ed.), *The art of effective facilitation: Reflections from social justice educators* (pp. 135–150). Sterling, VA: Stylus Publishing

Bell, D. A. (1973). *Race, racism, and American law.* Frederick, MD: Aspen Publishers.

Boomstrom, R. B. (1998). 'Safe spaces': reflections on an educational metaphor. *Journal of Curriculum studies, 30*(4), 397–408.

Crenshaw, K. (1991). Mapping the margins: Intersectionality, identity politics, and violence against women of color. *Stanford Law Review, 43*(6), 1241–1299. http://www.jstor.org/stable/1229039

Cross Jr, W. E. (1971). The negro-to-black conversion experience. *Black world, 20*(9), 13–27.

Delgado, R., & Stefancic, J. (1993). Critical race theory: An annotated bibliography. *Virginia Law Review, 79*(2), 461–516. doi:10.2307/1073418. https://www.jstor.org/stable/1073418

Freire, P. (1968). *Pedagogy of the oppressed.* New York, NY: Seabury Press.

Fulbright-Anderson, K., Lawrence, K., Sutton, S., Susi, G., & Kubisch, A. (2005). *Structural racism and youth development: Issues, challenges, and implications.* Washington, DC: The Aspen Institute.

Guerra, N. G., & Bradshaw, C. P. (2008). Linking the prevention of problem behaviors and positive youth development: Core competencies for positive youth development and risk prevention. In N. G. Guerra & C. P. Bradshaw (Eds.), *Core competencies to prevent problem behaviors and promote positive youth development. New Directions for Child and Adolescent Development, 122*, 1–17.

Helms, J. E. (1993). *Black and white racial identity: Theory, research, and practice*. Westport, CT: Praeger Publishers.

Ladson-Billings, G., & Tate, W. F. (1995). Toward a theory of culturally relevant pedagogy. *American Educational Research Journal, 32*(3), 465–491. DOI: 10.2307/1163320

Larson, R. W., & Walker, K. C. (2010). Dilemmas of practice: Challenges to program quality encountered by youth program leaders. *American Journal of Community Psychology, 45*(3–4), 338–349. DOI: 10.1007/s10464-010-9307-z

Perry, B. D., & Szalavitz, M. (2006). *The boy who was raised as a dog; and other stories from a child psychiatrist's notebook: What traumatized children can teach us about life, loss and healing*. Philadelphia, PA: Basic Books.

Sue, D. W., Capodilupo, C. M., Torino, G. C., Bucceri, J. M., Holder, A., Nadal, K. L., & Esquilin, M. (2007). Racial microaggressions in everyday life: Implications for clinical practice. *American Psychologist, 62*(4), 271. DOI: 10.1037/0003-066X.62.4.271

VeneKlasen, L., Miller, V., Budlender, D., & Clark, C. (2002). *A new weave of power, people & politics: the action guide for advocacy and citizen participation*. Oklahoma City, OK: World Neighbors.

Walker, K. C., & Larson, R. W. (2006). Dilemmas of youth work: Balancing the professional and personal. *New directions for Youth Development, 112*, 109–118.

CHAPTER 7

MAINTAINING MOMENTUM TO EMPOWER BOYS AND YOUNG MEN OF COLOR IN THE OUT-OF-SCHOOL TIME FIELD

Jon Gilgoff

Over a twenty year period I participated in the struggle to reduce disparities facing male youth of color and help facilitate successful life outcomes for an unjustly targeted and poorly supported population. My work in this area began in graduate school as a founder, community organizer, and co-leader of Columbia School of Social Work's Male Action Coalition (Gilgoff, 2001). Our group was founded in 1999 to address the need for greater awareness, programming, funding, research, and education dedicated to males, in particular, males of color.

My views have been formed as a social worker dedicated to the strength-based therapeutic empowerment of urban male youth. I have facilitated afterschool youth groups and coordinated civic engagement and youth advocacy events. I have written curricula, research papers, and training manuals. Observing the challenges faced by boys and young men of color (BYMOC) across decades and cities, I became committed to providing not only services grounded in social justice, but also therapeutically-informed community capacity building. The goal of my

Changemakers! Practitioners Advance Equity and Access in Out-of-School Time Programs,
pages 109–121.

work over the years is to help transform institutions to be more responsive to the needs of this population.

In this chapter I reflect on the extent to which targeted efforts to empower BYMOC have been implemented and institutionalized within the out-of-school-time (OST) field. In addition, I examine how this work is aligned with the broader movement to address the inequality that males of color endure as they face well-documented disparities in health, safety, educational, and socio-economic status (Davis, Kilburn, & Schultz, 2009). I will assess the road traveled and areas still in need of further exploration and collective action.

It is my belief that this chapter is particularly important given a momentous leadership transition—that which occurred in 2016 between the administrations of Presidents Obama and Trump. While the former established *My Brother's Keeper*, a first of its kind national cradle-to-college initiative for young men of color (Wise, 2016), Trump's form of masculinity, which some consider toxic, seeps not only into discriminatory rhetoric (Siebel, 2017) but also creates a policy platform seemingly designed to create greater societal inequity. Within this climate, the movement to empower BYMOC continues, and I intend this chapter to be a resource for ongoing efforts. The central question guiding this chapter is, to what extent have practices, programs, and policies supporting BYMOC become institutionalized and how can they be further embedded within the OST ecosystem?

The needs of BYMOC are complex—including disproportionate exposure to violence and punishment, exposure to teachers and health care practitioners who lack cultural competency, as well as a dearth of opportunities designed to engage youth who are disconnected from education (Bryant, Harris, & Bird, 2013). Community response therefore must be comprehensive at three levels: micro, mezzo, and macro. This chapter will address all three levels: a) micro: providers working directly with BYMOC; b) mezzo: OST staffing and cultural competency, and c) macro: institutional policies and procedures, funding priorities and practices, and ways researchers can view BYMOC as a priority population.

For each of these areas, I present strategies and examples. Many I have observed firsthand and others are drawn from research studies. I provide suggestions based on my experience as a practice-based researcher in the hope of being a resource for the next generation of change agents. I close the chapter with a formal call to action in an effort to motivate others to continue this movement.

SETTING THE CONTEXT

A man who pays respect to the past, paves the way for his own greatness
—*African proverb*

The Importance of Culture and Gender Exploration

As in the practice of developing boys into men, culturally responsive research begins with culturally-based honoring. As a white person working in communities of color, I aim to demonstrate the highest levels of respect and responsibility. To be an ally is not a static identity but an ongoing practice (Kivel, 2017). This, for me, began formally in the 1990s as a mentor within a rites of passage program led by African American men at the Washington, D.C. agency Sasha Bruce Youthwork. The model was based on the work of leading scholars of the Afrocentric movement, including Maulana Karenga who in 1966 created the holiday of Kwanzaa, and Jawanza Kunjufu, who launched the Simba program in Chicago that offered manhood training to develop solidarity and positive racial identity (Boyd, 2003). Such programs were established to help counteract the adverse effects of sociological and economic forces undermining the development and appropriate expression of masculinity among black males, particularly among people living in inner cities and from low-income backgrounds (Hunter & Davis, 1994).

Efforts to reconnect youth of color to cultural practices from which they have been disconnected by historical oppression and white supremacy are not exclusive to African Americans. The National Compadres Network (NCN) grew out of cultural circles, *or circulos* made up of Chicano, Latino, Native and Raza[1] men who came together with a commitment towards healing and honor. The *circulo* is an ancient tradition, used to pay respect to ancestors. Building on this practice, NCN created *Joven Noble*, a group work curriculum and evidence-based program that supports Latino males through the promotion of positive youth development and prevention of risky behaviors (Tello, Cervantes, Cordova, & Santos, 2010).

From Deficit to Assets

While early OST research was overwhelmingly on risk prevention (Dryfoos, 1990; Glasgow, 1981; Jessor & Jessor, 1977), over the last twenty years the focus has shifted to a strength-based approach emphasizing the assets youth and community institutions bring to the table. It challenges us to think beyond individual youth to a broader view, that of communities and institutions. Within BYMOC literature and programming, this shift from prevention-focused approaches to more holistic models integrating emotional health, empowerment, and exploration (Zeldin, 2000) has helped to address systemic barriers to academic achievement, economic mobility, and well-being (Littles, Bowers, & Gilmer, 2008; Noguera, 2008; Young, 2004).

Programmatically grounded in developing male identity and a brotherhood committed to healthy relationships, emerging initiatives combine mentoring and traditional healing with youth organizing and community advocacy. They effectively engage BYMOC and empower youth to advocate for equity-building policies (Simmons, 2017).

---

[1] Raza is a term that denotes the empowerment of people of Latino heritage particularly Mexican Americans. https://www.urbandictionary.com/define.php?term=Raza

MICRO LEVEL PRACTICE—CREATING SPACE FOR GENDER-SPECIFIC & GENDER-RESPONSIVE PROGRAMMING

Three prevailing strategies show promise for working with BYMOC in the OST context. These include 1) rites of passage and cultural practices 2) academic support and enrichment; and 3) policy/advocacy (Woodland, 2008; Gilgoff & Ginwright, 2015).

Rites of Passage and Cultural Practices

Rites of Passage (ROP) is a gender-specific modality used with groups of boys to help them transition into men (or girls transition into women). It focuses on restorative strategies rooted in culture and ethnicity. Whatever the background of the participant, ROP helps youth build ethnic pride, learn more about their history, and develop a worldview focused on community and living in harmony with other people and nature.

ROP programs often have a focus on mentoring and positive role models. Although research on the impact of same-sex versus cross-sex mentoring is not conclusive (Liang et al., 2013), nonprofit youth organizations often make an effort to pair boys with men. Some organizations only make same-sex matches (Big Brothers Big Sisters, 2014). For such agencies, and for families requesting a same-gendered mentor for male children, waiting lists are the norm. Indeed, the lack of male volunteers is one of the toughest challenges (Garringer, 2004).

For programs exclusively serving BYMOC, having staff and volunteers from similar backgrounds is a priority. One such program utilizing ROP as well as providing academic support, mentorship, health and wellness and career development is Latino Men and Boy's Program of The Unity Council (Community Crime Prevention Associates, 2012). Another gender-specific initiative which utilizes a ROP approach, this time through a multi-racial manhood development model, is the Brothers, UNITE! program of Brothers on the Rise[2].

Academics & Enrichment

Academic initiatives can help bridge the achievement gap, which, although greatest for African-American males (Kirp, 2010), also affects Latino males and other ethnic minorities. Academic support for older male youth often focuses on college preparation and integrates career readiness and/or vocational activities including paid internships. High-interest modalities such as sports, media, arts, and technology are enrichment strategies that can integrate skill building and vocational development. These are grounded in learning strategies particularly effective for males, that is, kinesthetically oriented and project-based approaches (Gurian & Stevens, 2011).

---

[2] In the spirit of full disclosure, I am the founder of this organization and served as the executive director from 2008–2016.

The two main staples of afterschool programming, academics and enrichment, are overwhelmingly delivered in mixed-sex groups. Mixed-sex groups offer an opportunity to integrate gender and culturally competent practices, and therefore impact BYMOC at a greater scale than strictly gender-specific modalities.

When working with mixed gender groups, youth workers must recognize that most communities of color have a strong focus on interdependence, summed up by the African proverb, "I am because we are" (Aguilar, 2015). One ritual used effectively by programs is a quote of the day or week, which can be adapted to highlight male and female leaders from various cultures through the recitation and analysis of ancient proverbs such as Spanish-language *dichos* and modern writing such as music which can have powerful lyrics that resonate with youth. In this way, exploration of gender can be integrated into OST groups of mixed male, female, trans and gender non-conforming youth, helping build awareness as well as empathy.

Policy/Advocacy Initiatives

Policy and advocacy strategies can engage BYMOC by exploring root causes of structural barriers to success, such as racism, poor quality schools, limited job opportunities, sentencing laws, and policing practices. Discussions about coping with obstacles can become a form of political education, contributing to "radical healing" (Ginwright, 2010). These strategies help to build awareness, engage youth in personal and political transformation through consciousness raising, action research, and, ultimately, organizing for change (See McGee's Chapter on Critical Youth Development in this book).

Working with African American youth, an organization called Leadership Excellence (now Flourish Agenda) fosters social change by creating pathways to social emotional well-being, healing and action so that urban youth can overcome racial trauma and the psycho-social harm they experience in their daily lives. They equip educators and youth service providers with curricula, training, and new technology to provide transformative learning experiences and leadership development to youth, leading to the creation of peaceful, supportive climates in neighborhoods and schools. Another organization, the Urban Strategies Council, partners with public agencies, grassroots organizing groups, and philanthropic organizations to catalyze lasting social change. The Council works with community stakeholders to build strategies and capacities for effective collective action and works to build partnerships and alliances across a wide array of community interests. At the same time, they are proactive in identifying issues that impact urban communities, building understanding of the issues, and crafting agendas to address those issues. For example, the Council has worked with local youth organizations to rally BYMOC around policy initiatives crafted by the Assembly Select Committee on the Status of Boys and Men of Color in California (2012).

MEZZO LEVEL PRACTICE—DEVELOPING AN OST WORKFORCE THAT IS RESPONSIVE TO THE NEEDS OF BYMOC

Mezzo level practices involve addressing the workforce and context in which BY-MOC participate. A 2006 workforce study indicates that OST workers are overwhelmingly female and white (National AfterSchool Association, 2006). While figures may have shifted since then, and in urban areas these percentages may be less extreme, it is fair to say we still have a serious demographic disconnect between BYMOC and providers. Although youth workers can effectively serve across differences, successful programs employ at least some staff members who represent participants' cultural backgrounds (Metz, Bandy, & Burkhauser, 2009). The need for more male mentors cannot be over-emphasized. This is especially true for the high number of children being raised in female single parent households including 42% of Latinos and 66% of African Americans (Kids Count Data Center, n.d.).

Recruiting Male Instructors of Color

The OST field can learn from school day education efforts to diversify their ranks with targeted recruitment efforts such as NYC Men Teach. This public-private partnership had the intention of putting 1,000 new men of color into the classroom by 2018. It is part of a citywide Young Men's Initiative, whose goals are to reduce disparities in health, education, and employment facing this population (Klein, 2016). Over its first two years between 2015 and late 2017, the initiative added 900 men of color into the teacher pipeline, and there were 350 more men of color in the classroom as a result of the initiative (Gonzalez, 2017).

The African American Male Achievement (AAMA) initiative was launched by Oakland Unified School District in 2010 and now is housed in the Office of Equity which also focuses on Latino and API males, female youth of color, and LGBTQ youth. Though AAMA clearly operates at both the micro and macro levels, it can also be highlighted at the mezzo level for bringing more African American men into the school day and afterschool settings. While the immediate impact has been focused on academics (AAMA youth now are achieving GPAs almost .5 higher than African American male youth not enrolled in the program), the initiative also has created more professional positions for African American men by certifying its instructors in Career Technical Education (Watson, 2014).

While efforts to diversify the school day and OST with more male instructors of color has clearly borne fruit, targeted recruitment may have limited success because of low wages and concurrent socialization for men to be breadwinners and high-income earners. Because of these pressures, male educators are vulnerable to feelings of inadequacy, depression, and a sense of loss around their masculinity (Eleni, 2017), and often choose other careers.

This dynamic points to a macro level systemic issue which needs attention—low compensation rates. With an average $25,540 annual salary for afterschool teachers (Glassdoor, n.d.) with part-time slots and no health benefits, turnover is high, and men look elsewhere. For example, although NYC Men Teach has brought many new men of color to the classroom, Gonzalez (2017) cites retention as an ongoing issue.

To address this challenge and bring additional funding into the OST field, California's successful Save After School Campaign engaged youth leaders as advocates to work alongside adult allies and political champions. With an additional 50 million dollars secured in 2017 for OST programs serving low income children (Fensterwald, 2017), this is a clear example of how systems change victories can spur progress on the micro and mezzo levels.

Training White Staff

Besides diversifying the OST field with more males of color, there is also a need for white professionals to effectively work across cultures (Bryant et al., 2016). My Brother's Keeper and MENTOR: The National Mentoring Partnership (n.d.) stress the importance of moving beyond cultural competence to the development of critical consciousness. In a critical stance, one never fully understands or becomes an expert on other people or their reality. Instead, the goal is to engage in deep listening and learning about the individual and the complex set of factors impacting their lives.

Brothers on the Rise, for example, matches the backgrounds of staff with participants. In addition, it provides training and technical assistance to institutions serving BYMOC in the areas of critical consciousness and culturally-based practices. The organization has also run annual learning communities to which youth organizations and school districts send their staff to learn how to implement gender-based curricula and other gender and culturally responsive practices.

MACRO LEVEL PRACTICE—INSTITUTIONALIZING ORGANIZATIONAL, FUND, AND POLICY DEVELOPMENT

While micro and mezzo level strategies address immediate challenges and provide supports, we must not lose sight of underlying and overarching structural inequities. Potential solutions must "address institutional racism, racial profiling, inadequate and under-resourced schools, homophobia, and political, economic and social oppression. Deep systemic and structural change is what is needed to transform the educational and employment outcomes" (Funders' Collaborative on Youth Organizing, 2015, pp. 3–4).

For organizations seeking to engage and empower BYMOC, there is a need to include them in developing and implementing strategies, to ground decisions in their expressed needs (Matthew & Ferber, 2016). In my experience, it has often been male youth of color who are the last to be engaged (or aren't engaged at all) in structured afterschool services but who could most benefit. Yet, they are seldom considered when deciding on program schedules, content, and overall recruitment and retention approaches (see the Loeper chapter in this book).

Organizational and Policy Development

Activities that appeal to BYMOC can also revolve around policy. For example, in BOTR youth engaged each year in dialogue with elected officials around policies and programs to address priority issues affecting them and their "brothers." Topics included community violence, homelessness, and police abuse, racial profiling, and the murder of unarmed men of color. For organizations serving younger youth—early engagement in macro-level political processes creates a pipeline for entry into more formal organizing with set campaigns and clear policy objectives. For younger youth, field trips to local government offices or visits from elected officials or their staff are critical in establishing a culture of civic engagement.

The Brothers, Sons, Selves Coalition is an organization that gathers testimony from Los Angeles youth through meetings and town halls and then presents the testimony to elected officials and other stakeholders along with suggested policy changes. One of many statewide groups that interacts with the California State Assembly Select Committee on the Status of Boys and Men of Color, they have contributed to the passage of numerous bills including Safe Neighborhood Grants, Learning Communities for School Success, College and Career Access Pathways partnerships, and a required reporting system for law enforcement agencies to report on peace officer incidents involving use of force (Alliance for Boys and Men of Color, n.d.).

Another strategy for empowering BYMOC is participating in community-wide coalitions focused on this cause, which can occur in OST programs that offer civic engagement activities. As part of the My Brother's Keeper Initiative, cities across the country answered former President Obama's call to action to create plans to catalyze greater equity for BYMOC. Stakeholders convened to review current policies and their impact. Groups crafted implementation strategies to address inequality, leveraging existing resources to support targeted outcomes (Philpart, Brown, & Masoud, 2015). While this model is not specific to OST, collaborations that involve multiple stakeholders from a given community or institution can be instructive for schools and agencies wishing to affect change. At Edna Brewer Middle School in Oakland, California, for example, an interdisciplinary team of teachers, administrators, counselors, security guards and OST staff, used a similar model of inquiry and organizing to address everything from school climate to gender and culturally responsive instruction.

Fund Development

The Executives' Alliance to Expand Opportunities for Boys and Men of Color has provided significant funding opportunities to serve this population. This prioritization of BYMOC within grant making has helped institutionalize programming and is key to ensuring sustainability. OST agency staff and youth participants can attend funders' strategic planning meetings and advocate for the needs of BYMOC so it gets embedded into Requests for Proposals (RFPs). The Fund for Children and Youth, a tax levy driven initiative, is a model for this type of proactive community engagement and responsive issue prioritization. They have also created a small and emerging category for grant seekers, which is important since as a relatively new field, emerging agencies serving BYMOC have less capacity and need more support to win grants when pitted against larger organizations (See the chapter by Rebecca Fabiano chapter in this book).

In a climate where so many oppressed populations are under attack and funders seek to address immediate needs, it is imperative that BYMOC-focused initiatives receive ongoing support to maintain momentum towards greater efficacy and equity. Indeed, foundations too often, "fail to do enough, early enough, to sustain sustainability" (Weiss, Coffman, & Bohan-Baker, 2002, p. 9).

CONCLUSION

There is an ongoing need for OST organizations to institutionalize gender-specific programming for BYMOC, ideally led by men from the same backgrounds. It is critical, however, that such programming be carefully and intentionally designed so that they do not compete with other high-interest offerings. Supplementing traditional academic and enrichment offerings with opportunities for leadership and community activism will help maintain the momentum achieved by the BYMOC movement. Through gender-specific groups and integration of gender and culturally responsive practices into all activities, the OST field can continue to grow its contribution to positive youth development.

OST organizations must join community efforts to advance racial, economic, environmental, and social justice—including universal health care, free college education, and criminal justice reform. On a national scale, the momentum achieved in the movement to empower BYMOC will continue to benefit from Obama's My Brother's Keeper initiative, which is sustained beyond his presidency through his Foundation (Holly, 2017). However, without a champion in the White House and with ongoing threats to the well-being of our society's most vulnerable, BYMOC will need allies from all corners and at all levels—micro, mezzo, and macro.

RESEARCH CONNECTIONS FROM THE EDITORS

As the evidence base on BYMOC grows, scholars and practitioners can build on current initiatives, including those that have been well studied within traditional education but less for OST. For example, school districts have been working to reduce the disproportionate impact of harsh discipline and zero tolerance policies on BYMOC such as suspension and expulsion. A research question worth pursuing might be whether OST programs implement harsh discipline and zero tolerance policies in the first place, and if not, why? Gaining the perspective of youth professionals on this topic would add value to the school-based research.

Restorative justice and mediation programs, first emerging in the school day, are now the focus of intense scrutiny and staff training in the OST context. Restorative Justice may be particularly useful in work with BYMOC, and implementation studies in the OST space may be quite revealing, and, again, add to the school-based research literature. Finally, school-day initiatives such as targeted recruitment for male providers of color and learning communities that build cultural responsiveness could be applied in the OST field. OST programs are quite intentional about (and successful in) hiring young men of color, which may provide a pipeline for them to either move up into OST administration or conversely into the school-day teaching fields. Research that examines this pipeline (whether "leaky" or not) is a worthwhile effort.

There are also particular subpopulations in need of attention. To date, African American and Latino males have been the focus of many studies. This is positive and has resulted in numerous research articles, syntheses, and compilations of resources for the OST field such as those included in the Latino Young Men and Boys Bibliography created by the Insight Center for Community Economic Development (n.d.). However, other groups are also unduly targeted by oppressive forces and therefore in need of equity-driven practices and research. Along those lines, Ahuja and Chlala (2013) call for more attention to Asian American and Pacific Islander and Arab, Middle Eastern, Muslim and South Asian populations. Additionally, studies of indigenous/Native Americans could help push the movement beyond the "black and brown" binary that can characterize some efforts. Finally, there is a need for inclusivity within the movement of queer and transgender identified BYMOC. This solidarity is part of the overall struggle to end sexism and homophobia, develop BYMOC as allies, and advocate for gender justice programs (Hoff Summers, 2000).

REFERENCES

Aguilar, E. (2015, February 25). Making connections: Culturally responsive teaching and the brain. *Edutopia*. Retrieved from https://www.edutopia.org/blog/making-connections-culturally-responsive-teaching-and-brain-elena-aguilar

Ahuja, S., & Chlala, R. (2013). *Widening the lens on boys and young men of color: California AAPI & AMEMSA perspectives*. San Francisco, CA: Asian Americans/Pacific Islanders in Philanthropy.

Alliance for Boys and Men of Color. (n.d.). *Alliance for Boys and Men of Color policy wins*. Retrieved from http://www.allianceforbmoc.org/take-action/state-campaign

Assembly Select Committee on the Status of Boys and Men of Color in California. (2012). *Claiming the promise of health and success for boys and men of color in California: Final report and policy platform for state action 2012–2018*. http://www.allianceforbmoc.org/resources/library/select-committee-final-recommendations-2012-2018

Big Brothers Big Sisters of Tucson. Admin. (2014, December 15). How gender effects youth mentoring relationships. *Big Brothers Big Sisters of Tucson, All Events, Blog.* Retrieved from https://www.tucsonbigs.org/gender-affects-youth-mentoring-relationships/

Boyd, F. N. (2003). *Black families in therapy: Understanding the African American experience.* New York, NY: The Guilford Press.

Bryant, R., Harris, L., & Bird, K. (2013*). Investing in boys and young men of color: The promise and opportunity.* Washington, D.C. & Princeton, NJ: Center for Law and Social Policy and Robert Wood Johnson Foundation.

Bryant, R., Harris, L., & Bird, K. (2016). Investing in boys and young men of color. *National Civic Review, 105*(1), 12–20.

Community Crime Prevention Associates. (2012). *Evaluation of Latino men and boys program.* Alameda, CA: Author.

Davis, L. M., Kilburn, M. R., & Schultz, D. J. (2009). *Reparable harm: Assessing and addressing disparities faced by boys and young men of color.* Santa Monica, CA: RAND.

Dryfoos, J. (1990). *Adolescents at risk: Prevalence and prevention.* New York, NY: Oxford University Press.

Eleni, E. (2017, June 25). The pressure on men to be providers is one reason they have much higher suicide rates. *Global News.* Retrieved from https://globalnews.ca/news/3550896/the-pressure-on-men-to-be-providers-is-one-reason-they-have-much-higher-suicide-rates/

Fensterwald, J. (2017, June 12). Gov. Brown agrees not to hold back money from California schools next year. *EdSource.* Retrieved from https://edsource.org/2017/gov-brown-agrees-not-to-hold-back-money-from-california-schools-next-year/583230

Funders' Collaborative on Youth Organizing and Movement Strategy Center. (2015). *Boys and Young Men of Color National Youth Table statement.* Retrieved from https://fcyo.org/resources/national-youth-alliance-for-boys-and-men-of-color-2015-statement-and-recommendations

Garringer, M. (2004). Putting the "men" back in mentoring. *National Mentoring Center Bulletin, 2*(2), 1–8. Retrieved from http://educationnorthwest.org/sites/default/files/resources/bulletin_male_recruitment.pdf

Gilgoff, J. (2001). The male action coalition of Columbia University School of Social Work: An example of successful community organizing. *The New Social Worker, 8*(4), 18–19.

Gilgoff, J., & Ginwright, S. (2015, Spring). Towards more equitable outcomes: A research synthesis on out-of-school-time work with boys and young men of color. *Afterschool Matters, 21*, 11–19.

Ginwright, S. A. (2010). *Black youth rising: Activism and radical healing in urban America.* New York, NY: Teachers College Press.

Glasgow, D. G. (1981). *The black underclass: Poverty, unemployment and entrapment of ghetto youth.* Thousand Oaks, CA: Jossey-Bass.

Glassdoor. (n.d.). *After school teacher salaries.* (Data file). Retrieved from https://www.glassdoor.com/Salaries/after-school-teacher-salary-SRCH_KO0,20.htm

Gonzalez, S. (2017, November 13). As city recruits male teachers of color, retention challenges persist. *WNYC News.* Retrieved from https://www.wnyc.org/story/new-york-city-recruits-male-teachers-of-color-retention/

Gurian, M., & Stevens, K. (2011). *Boys and girls learn differently: A guide for teachers and parents*. San Francisco, CA: Jossey-Bass.

Hoff Summers, C. H. (2000). *The war against boys. How misguided feminism is harming our young men*. New York, NY: Simon & Schuster Paperbacks.

Holly, D. (2017, September 7). My Brother's Keeper Merges with Obama Foundation. *Nonprofit Quarterly*. Retrieved from https://nonprofitquarterly.org/2017/09/07/brothers-keeper-merges-obama-foundation/

Hunter, A. G., & Davis, J. E. (1994). Hidden voices of black men: The meaning, structure, and complexity of manhood. *Journal of Black Studies, 25*(1), 20–40.

Insight Center for Community Economic Development. (n.d.). *Latino Young Men & Boys bibliography*. Retrieved from https://insightcced.org/latino-young-men-boys-bibliography/

Jessor, R., & Jessor, S. (1977). *Problem behavior and psychosocial development*. New York, NY: Academic.

Kids Count Data Center (n.d.). *Children in single-parent families by race.* (Data file). Retrieved from http://datacenter.kidscount.org/data/tables/107-children-in-single-parent-families-by#detailed/1/any/false/573,869,36,868,867/10,11,9,12,1,185,13/432,431

Kirp, D. L. (2010). Invisible students: Bridging the widest achievement gap. In C. Edley & J. R. de Velasco (Eds.), *Changing places: How communities will improve the health of boys of color.* (pp. 67–96). Berkeley & Los Angeles, CA: University of California.

Kivel, P. (2017). *Uprooting racism*. Gabriola Island, Canada: New Society Publishers.

Klein, R. (2016, July 25). There is a shortage of male teachers of color. NYC is working to fix that. *HuffPost*. Retrieved from https://www.huffingtonpost.com/entry/nyc-men-teach_us_578e7e40e4b07c722ebc8a22

Liang, B., Bogat, G. A., & Duffy, N. (2013). Gender in mentoring relationships. In *Handbook of Youth Mentoring* (pp. 159–174). SAGE Publications Inc. DOI: 10.4135/9781412996907.n11

Littles, M., Bowers, R., & Gilmer, M. (2008). *Why we can't wait: A case for philanthropic action: Opportunities for improving the live outcomes of African American males.* New York, NY: Ford Foundation.

Matthew, S., & Ferber, T. (2016). *Opportunity youth playbook: A guide to reconnecting boys and young men of color to education and employment.* Washington, DC: Opportunity Youth Network and the Forum for Youth Investment.

Metz, A., Bandy, T., & Burkhauser, M. (2009). *Staff selection: What's important for out-of-school time programs?* Washington, DC: Child Trends. Retrieved from https://www.childtrends.org/wp-content/uploads/2009/02/Staff-Selection.pdf

My Brother's Keeper and MENTOR: The National Mentoring Partnership (n.d.). *Guide to mentoring boys and young men of color*. Retrieved from www.mentoring.org/newsite/wp-content/.../05/Guide-to-Mentoring-BYMOC.pdf

National AfterSchool Association. (2006). *Understanding the afterschool workforce: Opportunities and challenges for an emerging profession*. Houston, TX: Cornerstones for Kids. Retrieved from http://www.cpshr.us/workforceplanning/documents/06.11_Underst_Aftersc_Wkfrce.pdf

Noguera, P. (2008). *The trouble with black boys and other reflections on race, equity, and the future of public education*. San Francisco, CA: Jossey-Bass.

Peppler, K. (2017). *The SAGE encyclopedia of out-of-school learning.* Thousand Oaks, CA: SAGE Publications, Inc.

Philpart, M., Brown, Jr., L., & Masoud, S. (2015). *Building place-based initiatives for boys and men of color and vulnerable populations: A community planning guide. Policy link.* Oakland, CA: Policy Link. Retrieved from http://www.policylink.org/sites/default/files/pl_brief_bmocguide_magcloud.pdf

Siebel, N. J. (2017). How to keep Donald Trump from spreading his toxic masculinity to future generations. *Time.* Retrieved from http://time.com/4877364/trump-boy-scouts-jamboree-toxic-masculinity/

Simmons, M. (2017). *How can we help boys and young men of color heal, grow, and thrive?* Robert Wood Johnson Foundation Culture of Health Blog. Retrieved from https://www.rwjf.org/en/culture-of-health/2017/04/how_can_we_help_boys.html

Tello, J., Cervantes, R. C., Cordova, C., & Santos, S. (2010). Joven Noble: Evaluation of a culturally focused youth development program. *Journal of Community Psychology, 38*(6), 799–811.

Watson, V. (2014). *The Black Sonrise: Oakland Unified School District's commitment to address and eliminate institutionalized racism. An evaluation report prepared for the Office of African American Male Achievement.* Oakland, CA: Oakland Unified School District.

Weiss, H., Coffman, J., & Bohan-Baker, M. (2002). *Evaluation's role in supporting initiative sustainability.* Cambridge, MA: Harvard Family Research Project.

Wise, M. (2016). My Brother's Keeper and Obama's mission to help young men of color. *The Undefeated.* Retrieved from https://theundefeated.com/features/my-brothers-keeper-and-obamas-mission-to-help-young-men-of-color/

Woodland, M. H. (2008). Whatcha doin' after school? A review of the literature on the influence of after-school programs on young black males. *Urban Education, 43*(5), 537–560.

Young, A. (2004). *The minds of marginalized black men: Making sense of mobility, opportunity and future life chances.* Princeton, NJ: Princeton University.

Zeldin, S. (2000). Integrating research and practice to understand and strengthen communities for adolescent development: An introduction to the special issue and current issues. *Applied Developmental Science, 4*(1), 2–10.

CHAPTER 8

ENGAGING IMMIGRANT FAMILIES IN OUT-OF-SCHOOL TIME ACTIVITIES

Andrés Henríquez and Sonia Bueno

Cultural institutions, like the New York Hall of Science (NYSCI), are uniquely positioned to involve the entire family in learning and exploration. When families, as well as youth, are involved in out-of-school time (OST) programs, youth come to programs more often and show more of the positive behaviors we want for them: strong academic performance, school engagement, and caring relationships (Little, 2013).

In the fall of 2016, NYSCI launched *NYSCI Neighbors*, a hyperlocal[1] initiative in Corona, Queens, New York that engages students, teachers, families, and community members in creative Science, Technology, Engineering and Math (STEM) learning. NYSCI works in deep partnership with the local school district, as well as non-profit organizations to run two programs under the umbrella of *NYSCI Neighbors*. These programs focus on low-income immigrant and first-generation families who comprise more than half of the population in Corona. Through Science Ambas-

---

[1] NYSCI's hyperlocal initiative is focused specifically in our local zip code 11368 in Corona and East Elmhurst, Queens.

Changemakers! Practitioners Advance Equity and Access in Out-of-School Time Programs,
pages 123–134.

sadors, the first program, we provide free out-of-school time STEM opportunities, college preparation, and career resources for youth and in the second program, the Parent University, we support parent engagement, learning, and leadership.

Due to increased pressure by U.S. Immigration and Customs Enforcement (ICE) police and anti-immigrant rhetoric from our nation's leaders, we are living in a time of great uncertainty for immigrant communities. NYSCI aspires to serve as an anchor institution for families in Corona; offering a safe and welcoming space, and using the museum's assets to provide greatly needed resources and opportunities at no cost for thousands of immigrant and first-generation children and their families. We carefully designed Science Ambassadors and Parent University to address an opportunity gap. That is, immigrant youth and families have limited access to science education which, over time, contributes to the underrepresentation of this population in STEM fields. Increasingly, STEM education and competencies are required for participation in the global workforce, but many people in the United States—particularly those in low-income immigrant and first-generation communities—are being left behind. Latin and Central American immigrants are not proportionately accessing STEM-related career and financial opportunities for advancement (Carnevale & Fasules, 2017). Understanding the social and cultural barriers to access, a concern for any cultural institution such as a museum, is critical to create programs that mitigate these factors and welcome visitors to take full advantage of resources.

In this chapter we identify strategies and program elements that speak to immigrant youth and families, demonstrate how to create opportunities that allow for more access and equity, and share lessons learned for other OST professionals who desire stronger relationships with immigrant youth and families in their communities.

BACKGROUND

Corona is in Community School District 24, one of the city's most crowded, with 56 schools serving over 60,000 English Language Learners and Title 1 students. Additionally, all local schools test below the state average in math and English Language Arts, and nearly all students are enrolled in free or reduced lunch programs. Corona is a vibrant community with a bustling commercial hub populated by locally owned businesses, ethnic restaurants, cultural institutions and organizations, and is often a first stop for newly arrived immigrants. Nearly two-thirds of the community is foreign-born, and more than 90% speak a language other than English. Like much of New York City, the borough of Queens has been a port of entry for many new immigrant groups over the years including Greek, Italian, and now Central and South American. Most residents are now Hispanic—primarily from Ecuador, Colombia, and Mexico, as well as other countries in Central and South America. Poverty rates in Corona are higher than in the rest of Queens, with more than 24% of households below the poverty line.

NYSCI has been a landmark cultural institution in Corona for over 50 years. As the museum's name suggests, we focus on STEM. NYSCI is a leader in the science museum field, recognized for its highly regarded exhibitions, programs, and products, all of which are informed by a instructional approach called Design-Make-Play. We use this approach to tackle concepts that are often the most difficult or abstract for learners to master, and that often lead them to lose their enthusiasm for STEM. The Design, Make, Play approach is grounded in five core principles:

1. *Putting people and play at the center.* NYSCI leverages learners' natural instincts to engage playfully with compelling ideas and materials.
2. *Positioning learners as creators.* We engage our visitors as creators and makers, not just consumers, of content, materials, and material objects.
3. *Tackling problems considered worth solving.* We support interest-driven problem solving in which learners actively shape the tasks they are working on.
4. *Cultivating divergent solutions.* Learners are encouraged to pursue problems that have no one right answer.
5. *Providing an open invitation.* Our activities present a low barrier to entry, a high ceiling of rich potential complexity, and a wide berth for the creative expression of ideas.

These defining characteristics of Design-Make-Play—open-ended exploration, imaginative learning, personal relevance, deep engagement and delight—are the ingredients that inspire passionate learners, critical thinkers, and active citizens (Honey & Kanter, 2013). Our transformative model is designed to invite broad participation from all visitors to the museum.

While STEM education and competencies are increasingly required for participation in the global workforce, many people in the United States—particularly those in low-income immigrant and first-generation communities—are being left behind. We have examined the roots of these barriers, and understand that much of their basis resides in social and cultural elements.

HISTORY OF NYSCI NEIGHBORS

NYSCI Neighbors is a museum-wide initiative that has the long-term commitment of NYSCI's CEO and board of trustees. It is a multifaceted program in which NYSCI collaborates with local stakeholders to build a rich ecosystem of STEM educational opportunities for educators, young people, and families. The program originally started in 2011, when NYSCI staff began developing community partnerships with the goal of countering summer learning loss among local students. In its first year, NYSCI Neighbors quickly enrolled 120 families and gave them access to museums in New York City, low-cost entry to NYSCI, and bilingual science demonstrations. In the following years, the program grew to 700 families, the number of community partners expanded including partnerships with 10 K–8 schools and their Parent Teacher Associations and Parent Coordinators.

The long-term goal of NYSCI Neighbors is to create a hyper-local initiative in a high-needs and highly aspirational community where immigrant and first-generation Americans are offered pathways out of poverty through a pipeline of STEM and career development programs. NYSCI Neighbors undertakes a two-generation approach: providing multiple strategies and key programmatic interventions where both the child and their parents or caregivers are engaged as learners and all the community stakeholders that have influence in a child's education are actively involved in their success and future outcomes.

NYSCI Neighbors was re-launched in 2016, and a Vice President of STEM Learning in Communities[2] joined the team to expand NYSCI's presence in the community and to establish a national coalition of similar organizations working to support STEM learning among first generation families. As this outward facing work got underway, NYSCI Neighbors continued to expand at the museum and throughout the community. Two programs that were started since the re-launch: (1) *Science Ambassadors*, an afterschool program serving children in the NYSCI Neighbors network of twenty community schools and local non-profits; and (2) *Parent University*, a series of STEM-focused parent programs where families have opportunities to increase their awareness of STEM career opportunities and to engage with tools and resources that they can use to help their children succeed.

SOCIAL AND CULTURAL BARRIERS TO ACCESS

Many of NYSCI's half a million yearly visitors are from New York City's greater metropolitan area. However, for many of the newcomer and first-generation families in our immediate community this may be their very first museum experience. This is complicated by the fact that next door to the museum is a Rocket Park that includes a Gemini-Titan II and a Mercury Atlas D rocket, some of the tallest structures in Corona. For many newcomers the NYSCI campus looks more like a military base or a federal agency—a frightening symbol for many of our families who may be undocumented immigrants. We created NYSCI Neighbors with the intention of overcoming these participation barriers. To do so, we embarked on a intentional process to understand the roots of the barriers. We gathered input from key stakeholders—parents, educators, community leaders—about what would help them to enter the museum, which some might consider a frightening and alien territory, and about their needs in order to better design the program.

We also took a number of steps to build trust with the community in an effort to get local families to come regularly to the museum. We hired Spanish speakers that live and were raised in in the community, we increased the number of partnerships that offer programs parents care about (e.g. family literacy, understanding your child's Individual Education Plan), and we worked closely with each of our local school's parent coordinators to spread the word about the ongoing offerings at NYSCI for parents and children.

---

[2]In the spirit of full disclosure, the VP is one of the authors of this chapter.

ENGAGING FIRST GENERATION IMMIGRANT COMMUNITIES

Traditionally parent engagement has focused on parents advocating for their children in schools. Parents who are newcomers to this country may receive support by school and other nonprofits, but it is often focused on immigrant rights and how to navigate the school system. However, improving child outcomes involves supporting families on a wide range of issues.

First generation immigrants tend to have high aspirations for themselves and their children. Immigrants in Corona bring with them what Carola and Suárez-Orozco (2001) in their groundbreaking study, *Children of Immigration* call "a sense of optimism that their hard work will open new opportunities" for them and their children. Corona's immigrant families are highly engaged in their children's education with district elementary schools routinely reporting 100% parent participation on report card days. Carola and Marcelo Suarez-Orazco also identified a split between aspirations and actual choices that grows over time as children encounter obstacles that make it difficult, if not impossible, for them to achieve their aspirations. NYSCI's work is intended to address this split in such a way that aspiration and choice are effectively coupled and parents and their children have the knowledge and opportunities required to embrace career and academic next steps in STEM fields.

Understanding Immigrant Families' Needs

Before we launched NYSCI Neighbors, we learned about the community through interviews and focus groups. We talked to community leaders, school district personnel, and members of the local clergy to understand the work they were doing with the community. Perhaps most importantly, we held a number of focus groups with parents at NYSCI in both Spanish and English. We recruited parents through schools and, as an incentive, offered a twenty-five dollar gift certificate to NYSCI's store. The goals of the focus groups were to learn how to build more trust with the community, to learn about parents' perspectives of their children's career aspirations, to learn ways in which parents navigate the K–12 school system and to learn about the needs of parents and how might our museum be more helpful. Finally, we asked what was most important in helping them as parents.

Our parents taught us four important lessons. First, *parents have high aspirations for their children and are committed to helping students' achieve their goals, but want to know how to help with actionable steps.* Families want their aspirations for their children to be validated and they want to know specific steps they can take to help realize their child's ambitions. Families also want to be in the driver's seat and learn how to support their children in STEM learning and academics in general. Parents need information that empowers them to be effective role models and to understand middle, high school, and college access processes.

Second, *parents want a place for the entire family where their culture is valued.* Parents want a place that is comfortable and accessible, where they can learn and have fun with their children and interact with people who speak their native language. They want a place where the *entire* family is welcome—multi-generation and multi-caretaker families are common in the community, and the culturally-based importance of *familia* cannot be understated. Parents want to be informed about the educational value of what their children are doing (e.g., connections to STEM subject matter, and learning skills like problem-solving, teamwork and critical thinking); and to know how science is connected to their cultural traditions and practices.

Third, parents emphasized that learning English is critical to understanding the larger culture. Parents are eager to learn English because it will help them pursue jobs and help navigate their day-to-day lives. Many first-generation students are English language learners and have double the amount of work since they have to both learn English and the language of science and mathematics (Short & Fitzsimmons, 2007).

Fourth, parents want more assistance in navigating the K–12 space. Parents feel disconnected from school and find it difficult to understand how to navigate the complex school system for their children. Parents shared that they are too intimidated to ask educators questions about their children's future educational and vocational trajectories.

We used these lessons to design NYSCI Neighbors and more specifically, Science Ambassadors and Parent University. We hoped to demonstrate to parents that we heard them, that we cared, and that our programs were intended for them.

SCIENCE AMBASSADORS

To date, NYSCI has registered 1,714 students into our Science Ambassador program representing 1,030 unique households from the local community. The OST program is designed to help our students become more engaged with STEM. Science Ambassadors is for students enrolled in kindergarten through grade eight. The program runs throughout the school year from October through June and families are welcomed, for free, Monday through Thursday afternoons from 2:00 p.m. to 5:00 p.m (Note: with the exception of some free hours Fridays and Sunday, families and children pay to enter the museum). At present, every single one of our Science Ambassadors are from immigrant families and the majority (74%) are in kindergarten through second grade. Engaging so many immigrant youth at an early age is a powerful strategy for narrowing opportunity gaps.

Our local families place a high priority on learning and for many, their views of learning and education are very traditional and didactic[3]: workbooks and worksheets, homework drills, and many other traditional forms of learning. The Science Ambassadors program challenges that traditional notion of learning by engaging youth and parents in hands-on, experiential science and providing parents

---

[3] It is likely that this view of learning is brought with families in their experiences of school in their home countries, which may be more "formal," i.e. didactic and teacher-centered.

with the resources and support they need to engage their children in imaginative learning and education. Science Ambassadors participate in our Design-Make-Play pedagogical approach through a variety of activities. In addition, students receive homework help, explore NYSCI exhibits, solve engineering problems and learn new tools in workshops at our *Design Lab* and Maker Space, listen to science stories, and learn from live science demonstrations. As one parent put it:

> One of the best things about this program is spending more time with my daughter and nephews because, honestly, at home, they grab the phone and their tablet. But here, we spend time together and they teach us a program about where water comes from and I honestly never thought that it's like that and well, I was surprised that we learned so much today.

Exposing youth to STEM careers is critical to improve representation of immigrants in STEM Fields. To this end, we encourage our Science Ambassadors who are in middle school to attend STEM Career Nights which are held once a month during the school year. In this program, large and well-known STEM companies such as IBM, Pepsico, Con Edison (our local utility company), and United Airlines send representatives to talk to young people and parents about different career pathways into STEM. The STEM professionals also talk to youth about the kinds of choices they should be making now to prepare them for a STEM career. It is too early to know how many of our Science Ambassadors will pursue STEM careers but we do know they will not enter fields they do not know exist.

PARENT UNIVERSITY: DESIGNING NEW SERVICES BASED ON FAMILIES' NEEDS

Parent University, not to be confused with a degree granting institution, is a set of programs and activities that take place during the school year and uses a variety of strategies to increase parents' awareness of STEM and offer tools and resources to parents that will help their children achieve academic and career success.

Parent University is comprised of four distinct programs (see Figure 8.1) that are offered throughout the school year: Parent Ambassadors, Critical Transitions, Multi-Cultural Programming, and Empowering Parents. The programs use a two-generation approach—for children AND families—to provide STEM programs that focus on creativity and hands-on exploration. Parent University offers activities across multiple venues and settings including parent association meetings, local schools, and other community institutions (e.g. parks) to foster student success and position learning as a shared experience. It also gives local immigrant parents and families a voice and a platform to ensure their concerns, challenges, and stories are heard throughout the district, city, and nation. Below, we describe how we work with parents in each of the four components of Parent University.

Parent Ambassadors. Through this program parents have the opportunity to learn about STEM concepts in a hands-on science center environment and grow as leaders and STEM advocates in their community. Our Parent Ambassadors pro-

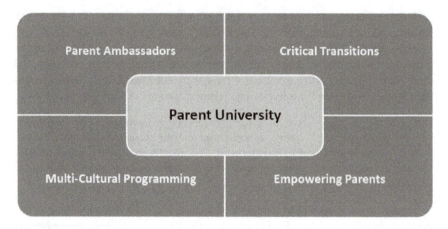

FIGURE 8.1.

gram runs for ten weeks and is held on Fridays from 3:00 pm—4:30 pm. Our main goal is to have parents become familiar with and comfortable in NYSCI and for them to learn through a hands-on, exploratory approach, rather than a traditional academic approach. Throughout the ten sessions, parents explore different areas of NYSCI including: *Connected Worlds*, a large-scale immersive installation composed of six interactive ecosystems connected together by a 3,000 square foot interactive floor and a 45-foot-high waterfall spread out across the walls of our famous Great Hall; our *Design Lab* which consists of five visually and thematically distinct activity areas and encourages visitors to be creative while experimenting with structures, circuits, simple materials and more; and our *Maker Space*, which is designed to foster creative problem solving through materials exploration and tinkering. Our parents keep a journal to jot reflections that help guide their thought process during each of the sessions. At the end of each session, we invite parents to reflect on how the theme of the day connected to their children's lives, their school work, and even their own past learning experiences.

Critical Transitions. Navigating New York City's K–12 system is complex even for the most involved families. For first generation parents and students who are undocumented it is doubly challenging and our parents shared with us that they desired assistance navigating the K–12 educational system. Critical Transitions creates a "patchwork" of support services for immigrant families. We work with institutional partners to provide families with a range of services, in linguistically and culturally inclusive settings. This patchwork of services helps them to navigate critical schools transitions, such as starting middle school or entering college, and to take advantage of opportunities available at high schools, colleges, and businesses (Enriquez, 2011). For example, we work with the Hispanic Federation who offers *Pathways to Academic Excellence*, a series of workshops that enables our parents to support their children in education from elementary to high school.

Parent Empowerment Opportunities. This program empowers parents by offering courses and opportunities in collaboration with partners like the NYC Department of Education's Adult and Continuing Education. Over the last year our parents have been enrolled in a STEM-focused English as a second language class that takes place two mornings a week at NYSCI's library. This course directly addresses parents' desire to learn English and it also introduces them to STEM vocabulary that they can use with their children.

Multicultural Programming. By focusing on families' culture and strengths, families see NYSCI as a place for them, one that honors STEM in diverse cultural contexts. Each year, we hold a number of community events including a community pop-up during our annual Maker Faire in the fall. The community pop-up allows our network of schools and parents to participate in the Maker Faire free of charge. At the end of the year we hold a culminating event and award ceremony that recognizes our Parent Ambassadors who have completed their classes as well as partners in our network. We also hold an annual community fair that features cultural dances and popular cuisine from multiple countries such as Ecuador, Mexico, Colombia and the Dominican Republic. The community fair also includes information about local schools, funders, and community organizations to introduce families to available resources.

LOOKING TOWARD THE FUTURE

We started Science Ambassadors and Parent University because we saw an opportunity for immigrant youth and families to tap into the multiple possibilities inherent in STEM fields and to use the rich resources that New York's cultural institutions offer. We adopted a growth mindset as we implemented each of the programs. We knew going in that we had much to learn. We found that to meaningfully engage immigrant families we had to first seek to understand their realities. We created structures and opportunities to inform our thinking and program designs, such as interviewing key stakeholders in churches, schools, and other community institutions. Most importantly, we talked with parent to ascertain their hopes and fears. We learned that embracing the cultural assets and strengths of our families is critical. This is why we cater our programs to multigenerational families, offer programming in Spanish, and partner with other organizations that value our families. Another key lesson is that we have to make the connections between our work and children's success explicit for both youth and families. This is the impetus for parents keeping a journal and for children and youth to be guided in discussions about how the activities will help them to reach their academic and vocational goals. This reflective and intentional process, in and of itself, helps parents and youth bridge the aspiration gaps.

Coalition for a STEM Future

Over the next year, we are taking what we are learning from NYSCI Neighbors to build the Coalition for a STEM Future that will bring together a national community of researchers and practitioners who are working to engage immigrant and first-generation families in STEM learning. These partners—selected based on the exemplary programs they offer and their commitment to improvement—will delineate common aims and successful practices for science centers and museums in promoting family engagement and supporting young people's STEM learning in immigrant and first-generation families. The Coalition will build a shared framework anchored in laudable local practices that have relevance for similar programs and institutions across the nation and will be a model of creative STEM engagement.

The work of the Coalition for a STEM Future will be anchored in the methodologies of a Networked Improvement Community. A NIC is a research structure that joins the discipline of improvement science with the powerful capacities of networks to foster innovation and social learning (Bryk, Gomez, & Grunow, 2010). The NIC structure reverses the usual top-down approach of research and development (R&D), amplifying promising ideas from on-the-ground practitioners. Participants can address an enduring problem with renewed vigor, breaking down silos and testing potential solutions quickly by leveraging the information-sharing capacities of the network. NIC methodologies have been identified as effective to use when the motivation driving the research is a desire both to *improve practices* and to *build capacity for continued improvement* across organizations who are working toward common goals, but may pursue them in widely varying, and previously unstudied, ways (Bryk, Gomez, Grunow, & LeMahieu, 2015; Deming, 2000).

NYSCI will engage the Carnegie Foundation for the Advancement of Teaching (CFAT)—the organization that pioneered the use of the NIC methodology in the field of education—to guide the launch of the NIC research community. Figuring out how science centers and museums can better connect immigrant and first-generation families with opportunities for STEM learning and careers is the type of high-priority, high-leverage problem the NIC approach is well-suited to address. To date, NIC methodologies have been used primarily to support improved practice in K–12 schools and universities. The Coalition will be one of the first opportunities to apply the methods of NICs to the informal education space, providing a significant opportunity to expand the reach and impact of this approach by applying it to out-of-school time settings.

We are looking forward to starting this project next year and collaborating with the Coalition of museums working with first generation immigrant families. In addition to partnering with CFAT The project will also enlist the support of Dr. Carola Suárez-Orozco and the Association of Science-Technology Centers

(ASTC). Our partners in the network will include the Arizona Science Center, Explora, Exploratorium, Houston Children's Museum, and The Tech.

RESEARCH CONNECTIONS

STEM is a hot topic in education and has been for quite a while due to the rapid advances in the field and the number of related STEM jobs that will be in demand in the future. The Every Student Succeeds Act of 2015 prioritizes STEM by offering academic enrichment grants to promote STEM learning with an emphasis on connecting experiences in and out of school (Afterschool Alliance, n.d.). However, there is clearly an opportunity gap where new immigrant children and youth are concerned, and this situation needs to be addressed in order to promote equity. Andrés Henriquez and Sonia Bueno demonstrate how powerful engaging entire families can be for STEM learning in out-of-school time contexts. Their emphasis on immigrant families is both timely and timeless. As noted by Kathryn Sharpe earlier in this volume, the demographics in the US are changing and to stay relevant OST programs must respond to the needs of increasingly diverse communities. While Corona was always a port for new immigrants, the population currently arriving from Central and South America are unlike their predecessors in that they have vastly different experiences of immigration, often escaping from war-torn countries and/or escaping drug violence. However, they are coming with other types of social capital, what Yosso (2005) calls "aspirational capital" referring to the ability to maintain hopes and dreams for the future, even in the face of real and perceived barriers" (p. 10).

The Coalition for a STEM Future is an impressive example of a research-practice connection. There are a number of questions that the Coalition, or others, interested in engaging immigrant families can explore. A starting point could be describing effective models for engaging immigrant families asking, what are key aspects of multicultural STEM learning? What approaches encourage multi-generational involvement? What are common barriers to involvement for youth and adults? What resources (partnerships, materials, funding) are needed to build, maintain, and grow programming using innovative engagement strategies for immigrant families? The field would also benefit from asking questions about how youth and families change in their perspectives, habits, and mindsets after participating in innovative STEM learning experiences. Questions such as how are parents' notions of learning/constructs changed through hands-on engagement in STEM? What additional educational resources do parents begin to use with their children? What actions do youth and families take to bridge the gap between aspiration and education-related choices? At a more systems level, the field may also begin to examine what expertise and resources OST programs bring to networks, coalitions and other large scale community efforts. Understanding the value-add of OST programs is critical to shifting the power imbalance that OST programs experience in partnerships (see Ken Anthony's chapter in this book).

REFERENCES

Afterschool Alliance. (n.d.). *Opportunities for expanded learning programs in ESSA*. Washington, DC: Author. Retrieved from: http://www.afterschoolalliance.org/documents/ESSA-Opportunities-for-Afterschool.pdf

Bryk, A. S., Gomez, L. M., & Grunow, A. (2010). *Getting ideas into action: Building networked improvement communities in education*. Stanford, CA: Carnegie Foundation for the Advancement of Teaching. Retrieved from http://www.carnegiefoundation.org/spotlight/webinar-bryk-gomez-building-networkedimprovement-communities-in-education

Bryk, A., Gomez, L., Grunow, A., & LeMahieu, P. (2015). *Learning to improve: How America's schools can get better at getting better*. Cambridge, MA: Harvard Education Publishing Group.

Carnevale, A. P., & Fasule, M. L. (2017). *Latino education and economic progress: Running faster but still behind*. Washington, DC: Georgetown University Center on Education and the Workforce.

Deming, W. (2000). *Out of the crisis*. Cambridge, MA: MIT Press.

Enriquez, L. (2011). "Because we feel the pressure and we also feel the support": Examining the educational success of undocumented immigrant Latina/o students. *Harvard Educational Review, 81*(3), 476–500.

Honey, M., & Kanter, D. E. (Eds.). (2013). *Design, make, play: Growing the next generation of STEM Innovators*. New York, NY: Routledge.

Little, P. (2013). Engaging families in afterschool and summer programs: A review of the research. In T. Peterson (Ed.), *Expanding minds and opportunities: Leveraging the power of afterschool and summer learning for student success*. Retrieved from: https://www.expandinglearning.org/expandingminds

Ma, Y., Lutz, A. (2018). Jumping on the STEM train: Differences in high school math and STEM college degree attainment between children of immigrants and natives in the United States. *Research in Sociology of Education, 20*, 129–154.

Short, D., & Fitzsimmons, S. (2007). *Double the work: Challenges and solutions to acquiring language and academic literacy for adolescent English language learners—A report to Carnegie Corporation of New York*. Washington, DC: Alliance for Excellent Education.

Suárez-Orozco, C., & Suárez-Orozco, M. M. (2001). *Children of immigration*. Cambridge, MA: Harvard University Press.

Yosso, T. J. (2005). Who's culture has capital? A critical race theory discussion of community cultural wealth. *Race Ethnicity and Education, 8*, 1. Retrieved from https://doi.org/10.1080/1361332052000341006

PART IV

SUMMARY AND CONCLUSION

SUMMARY AND CONCLUSION

Sara Hill and Femi Vance

In this book we set out to explore how access and equity play a role in quality experiences for youth, and, in particular, how the field has yet to meet the needs of the most underserved communities. Each chapter, and the issues raised—funding, outreach, relationships between institutions—were viewed with an access and equity lens. Within these broad topics, the book raises equity and access challenges as well as proposes solutions from the perspective of practitioners.

While many of the strategies identified in the book were designed and implemented with specific programs and youth in mind, there are many which are cross-cutting and can easily be adopted and adapted by other agencies and programs. For example, "close touch" and targeted outreach (see Loeper's chapter) are simple and effective strategies that help to ensure that parents and families become engaged and that an organization remains aligned to its mission. Becoming cognizant that many families and youth have experienced trauma can help agencies tailor specific types of professional development for staff (see chapters by Loeper and McGee). Learning how to create and sustain a city-wide network can be applied to any municipality (see chapter by Anthony). Recognizing the benefits and drawbacks of specialized versus generalized programs designed to serve youth with disabilities, and ways to be more inclusive can be a valuable exercise in any agency (see chapter by Stolz). We hope that the strategies presented in this book can be implemented at other youth organizations to reduce inequity

Changemakers! Practitioners Advance Equity and Access in Out-of-School Time Programs,
pages 137–140.
Copyright © 2019 by Information Age Publishing

137

and improve the experiences of youth at these programs and ultimately their life trajectories.

There are several ways that organizations and individual OST professionals can use this book (either individual chapters or in its entirety) to inform their equity and access efforts. For example, it can be used in a professional learning community to spark discussion about equity and access issues and/or OST professionals may use it to advocate within their organizations for more intentional and institution-wide practices. For those organizations and OST professionals primed for action, they may immediately implement and/or modify strategies within their contexts or use the chapters as a springboard to examine and make changes in their current policies and practices.

BUILDING OST CAPACITY

A major cross-cutting theme in the chapters is the need for professional development. The message is clear: to implement equitable programs and improve access to high-quality services we must better equip our staff. Authors in this book suggest that professional development should cover a range of topics that we have not seen as those typically provided for youth professionals—e.g., developing inclusive programs, trauma-informed care, creating and sustaining programing for boys and young men of color and programs which explore social identities.

Providing adequate professional development is easier said than done. The OST field has yet to discover the most effective approach to training OST professionals. One-time workshops are still the norm despite little evidence that this strategy helps OST professionals change their practices (Hill, Connolly, Akiva & McNamara, 2017). And OST programs must constantly weigh the pros and cons of investing in staff who may soon move onto another job. Cohort-based learning, particularly for those staff who are committed to the field, should perhaps be the next wave of professional development. Finally, colleges need to invest in OST professional pathways (both certificate programs and credit-bearing degrees) whose content is based on practices and research identified in the field.

Professional learning communities (PLCs) hold great promise. There is some evidence that PLCs boost participant learning and can lead to changes in practice (Vance, Salvaterra, Michelsen, & Newhouse, 2016). In addition, ongoing learning in cohorts provides opportunities for youth professionals to engage in inquiry into their practice and to assume leadership positions (Hill et al., 2017). The field has also seen some success in using site-based teams to further staff learning about program quality and continuous quality improvement processes. Popularized by the David P. Weikart Center, this strategy can be adopted to address concerns about equity and access. For example, site-based teams or working groups can focus on critical topics—such as creating brave spaces for youth and staff or recruiting and supporting male instructors of color.

RESEARCH-PRACTICE PARTNERSHIPS

At the end of each chapter in this book, we attempted to bridge the research-practice gap by generating discussion and questions to spur subsequent research studies. These questions are "ecologically valid" (Agee, 2009). This means that the questions are relevant to multiple OST settings and a wide swath of OST professionals because they have sprung directly from dilemmas in the field for which answers are needed.

CROSS-CUTTING QUESTIONS

We have identified several cross-cutting and broad questions for both researchers and practitioners that, if explored, can stimulate new approaches to advancing equity and access. These questions can also ground and guide meaningful partnerships between researchers and practitioners. They include:

- How can we break down the silos that create and maintain power imbalances in the out-of-school time field?
- Which policies support and which policies hinder efforts to increase equity and access in the out-of-school time field? These include policies at the program, local, state, and national level.
- How can youth and their families be involved in efforts to improve equity and access in programs?
- How do we empower and equip individuals within OST organizations to challenge norms and practices that perpetuate inequities and limit access to much needed programs?

We encourage researchers to engage with practitioners as well as youth about these questions and others like them so that the field can move toward more applied research. We need to provide opportunities that engage both researchers and practitioners in dialogue about the issues of equity and access. For example, national organizations for youth professionals (e.g. National AfterSchool Association, Afterschool Alliance) might host access and equity strands at conferences or host forums or roundtables that would bring together researchers and practitioners in structured discussions on these topics. We can embed issues of equity and access into continuous quality improvement or use a "case consultancy" approach used by the School Reform Initiative[1] on how to tackle emerging dilemmas.

The issues of access and equity are all clearly articulated by the authors in this volume. The next move is ours.

---

[1] To learn more, visit: http://schoolreforminitiative.org/doc/consultancy.pdf

REFERENCES

Agee, J. (2009) Developing qualitative research questions: A reflective process. *International Journal of Qualitative Studies in Education, 22*(4), 431–447. DOI: 10.1080/09518390902736512

Hill, S. L., Connolly, J., Akiva, T., & McNamara, A. R. (2017). Taking it to a new level: Inquiry-based professional development as a field building enterprise. In H. J. Malone & T. Donahue (Eds.), *The growing out-of-school time field: Past, present, and future* (pp. 115–132). Charlotte, NC: Information Age Publishing.

Vance, F., Salvaterra, E., Atkins Michelsen, J., & Newhouse, C. (2016). Professional learning communities: An alternative to the one-stop workshop. In K. M. Pozzoboni & B. Kirshner, (Eds.), *The changing landscape of youth work* (pp. 147–165). Charlotte, NC: Information Age Publishing.

BIOGRAPHIES

EDITORS

Sara Hill has over 25 years of experience in youth development, curriculum and instruction, nonprofit management, evaluation and research. She was a team member on a Department of Education funded project documenting 21st Century Community Learning Centers, and was a validator on a national project documenting promising practices in community colleges supporting low skills students. Dr. Hill has designed and delivered professional development for hundreds of educators at all levels, including youth and staff at community based organizations, public school teachers and administrators. She previously worked at the Partnership for Afterschool Education, the Robert Bowne Foundation, and as a consultant to the National Institute on Out-of-School Time and the National Writing Project. She received her M.Ed from Harvard University School of Education and her Ed.D. from Vanderbilt University, Peabody College.

Femi Vance, Ph.D. is a researcher at American Institutes for Research (AIR) where she researches and evaluates out-of-school time programs and provides technical assistance to youth development professionals. She has expertise in youth program quality, social and emotional learning, evaluation capacity build-

Changemakers! Practitioners Advance Equity and Access in Out-of-School Time Programs, pages 141–000.
141

ing, and skill-building in youth programs. She strives to translate her research into practice. She has co-authored practical guides for OST practitioners: Strategies to Promote Non-Cognitive Skills: A Guide for Educators and Youth Developers and Leading the Way to a Successful Professional Learning Community. She has extensive experience providing professional development to OST practitioners on a range of topics such as continuous quality improvement, engaging youth, and coaching staff. She is currently a National Summer Learning Field Consultant and she serves on the board of the California School Age Consortium. Dr. Vance holds a Master's in Public Policy from Johns Hopkins University and a Ph.D. in Educational Policy from UC Irvine.

CONTRIBUTORS

Ken Anthony is the Director of Professional Development and Research for the Connecticut After School Network. Being in the field for the past 27 years, Ken has worked as a front line staff, site supervisor, program director, district coordinator, to his current position for the past ten years. His primary role at the Network is to oversee training, professional and leadership development, program consultation, quality advising, and support research efforts. Ken holds a Bachelor's degree in Psychology with a concentration in Child Development from Southern Connecticut State University; a Master's degree in Human Services with a concentration in Organizational Management & Leadership from Springfield College, and was part of the inaugural class of White-Riley-Peterson Policy Fellows. Ken completed his Doctorate in Educational Leadership at the University of Hartford in 2015, where he researched expanded learning practices that build sustainable relationships and partnerships between school and afterschool program staff. This is a topic that he is passionate about and presents to state and national audiences frequently.

Sonia Bueno is a first-generation Latina who has worked in both formal and informal education at various local cultural institutions and public schools since 2007. Sonia is passionate about bringing equitable opportunities in education to underserved families. At NYSCI, Sonia focuses on providing parents with resources and learning opportunities that will allow them to become advocates for their children's education. Sonia holds a BA in Psychology/General Linguistics from Queens College and a Masters in teaching English to speakers of other languages (TESOL) from Hunter College.

Rebecca Fabiano, MSEd is a system-thinker who effectively leverages the assets of individuals and institutions to reach common goals. For nearly 25 years, she has worked in various capacities across nonprofit and youth-serving organizations, served on boards and helped to build solid youth programs that engage, encourage, and create spaces for positive development.

Jon Gilgoff is a bilingual Spanish speaking Licensed Clinical Social Worker with over twenty-five years working alongside diverse communities as a provider, trainer, consultant, supervisor and administrator within the fields of counseling, conflict resolution and youth development. He is founder and former Executive Director of the award-winning Oakland-based nonprofit Brothers on the Rise (BOTR), which continues to empower boys and young men of color, their adult allies and the institutions which serve them. Jon is a certified mediator, published writer and recipient of a Jefferson Award for Public Service. His work has appeared in The New Social Worker, Afterschool Matters, Newsday, and 99 Poets for the 99 Percent. He has held fellowships with Progressive Jewish Alliance (now Bend the Arc), LeaderSpring and Lead East Bay. Jon received his B.A. from Tufts University in International Relations and a Master's in Social Work from Columbia University. Jon currently works for the Equal Opportunity Department of Santa Clara County, trains with A Better Way and Fred Finch Youth Center, teaches at Holy Names University and is an Alameda County Public Health Commissioner.

Andrés Henríquez. Currently leading the NYSCI Neighbors initiative, a partnership between NYSCI and the local community, Andrés Henríquez brings a broad expertise to this position. Andrés worked previously as a program officer at both the National Science Foundation and the Carnegie Corporation of New York, where he launched a national program to develop the field of adolescent literacy. He was a key contributor to the National Research Council's Framework for K–12 Science Education, and the funding of Achieve Inc. to develop the framework-aligned Next Generation Science Standards.

Earlier in his career at the Center for Children and Technology, he was part of the community transformation in Union City, N.J., where he lead a partnership between Bell Atlantic and the Union City Schools, which received national recognition from President Clinton and Vice President Gore.

Rachel Loeper, co-founder and current education director at Mighty Writers, has taught ESL, remedial reading and creative writing. The mission of MW is to teach kids in Philadelphia and Camden, ages 7 to 17, to think and write with clarity so they can achieve success at school, at work and in life. They make every child feel welcomed, celebrated and Mighty by creating communities that are supportive, nurturing and striving. In 2011, the Pennsylvania Statewide Afterschool Network honored her as an Afterschool Champion. She served as an Afterschool Matters Fellow with the National Institute on Out-of-School-Time from 2010–12 and published, "Combat Sports Bloggers, Mad Scientist Poets and Comic Scriptwriters: Engaging Boys in Writing on Their Own Terms," (Afterschool Matters, Spring 2014). She currently serves on the Board of Wissahickon Charter School in the Mt. Airy neighborhood of Philadelphia. She received a BA in English Literature

& Writing from Goucher College, Baltimore, MD, and an MFA in Creative Writing from Hollins University, Roanoke, VA.

Merle McGee's passion for social justice was nurtured by her family since childhood, but it was after college that she committed herself to the nonprofit sector during the height of the AIDS crisis in NYC. For the past 20 years Merle has fought alongside historically marginalized and excluded communities for dignity, racial, gender and economic justice. She has extensive experience in nonprofit management, youth development, experiential learning and equity and inclusion. She has supported young people's development in many capacities including in direct service and senior leadership roles. Merle is particularly honored to have served as program leader for an award-winning college preparatory organization based in Upper Manhattan. She is passionate about building strong and effective multiracial and intergenerational teams and fostering humanistic and equitable communities where every person can fulfill their potential.

Merle received her B.F.A. from the Tisch School at New York University and holds a M.S. in Non-Profit Management from the Milano School of International Affairs, Management and Urban Policy at New School University. She is co-facilitator for the Undoing Racism Nonprofit Executives Collective, and a co-founder of The BIPOC Project, an antiracist collective committed to building solidarity among people of color and dismantling Native invisibility, Anti-Black racism and white supremacy. She been a Robert Bowne, Coro-Leadership NY and CoreAlign fellow focused on youth development, leadership, race and gender justice. Merle remains a humble practitioner of Capoeira Angola (an Afro Brazilian martial art).

Kathryn Sharpe is an Extension Educator with the University of Minnesota Extension Center for Youth Development, based in the Twin Cities metro area. Her primary focus in youth development is on advancing cultural competence and equity through efforts such as a statewide Diversity and Inclusion cohort and a Cultural Exchange program that she piloted, and on building the capacity of caring adults to work with young people through youth worker and volunteer training. In addition, Kathryn has led the development of many civic engagement/youth leadership clubs and experiences focused on engaging traditionally underserved communities, especially immigrant communities. Her graduate research in human geography focused on immigration and social movements. Through 4-H, she seeks to provide youth with opportunities to discover their own passions and to enlarge their sense of what is possible in life.

Suzanne Stolz, Ed.D. serves as an Assistant Professor of Special Education at the University of San Diego. A former high school English teacher, administrator, and leader of disability programs, she has expertise in online instruction, curriculum design, mentoring, school culture, Universal Design for Learning, and disability studies. She has created curriculum for OST providers and for disability mentoring. Suzanne has presented her research related to conceptions of disability and identity development of disabled students, which often includes reflection about her experience as a disabled student, at national and international conferences. She currently serves on the board of Society for Disability Studies. Suzanne is especially passionate about working with teachers to rethink their conceptions of disability and create inclusive school communities.

Sarah Zeller-Berkman, PhD is the Director of Youth Studies Programs at the CUNY School of Professional Studies. At CUNY SPS, she oversees the MA and Advanced Certificate in Youth Studies programs and directs the Intergenerational Change Initiative (ICI), which involves youth and adults in participatory action research projects related to intergenerational policy-making. Dr. Zeller-Berkman has spent the last two decades as a practitioner, researcher, evaluator, and capacity-builder in the field of youth and community development. Trained in Social-Personality Psychology, she has worked in partnership with young people on participatory action research projects about issues that impact their lives such as sexual harassment in schools, incarceration, parental incarceration, and high-stakes testing. Her publications include articles and chapters in the Journal of Community, Youth and Environments, The Handbook of Qualitative Research, AfterSchool Matters, New Directions for Evaluation, Globalizing Cultural Studies, and Children of Incarcerated Parents.

CPSIA information can be obtained
at www.ICGtesting.com
Printed in the USA
JSHW010015080220
4107JS00003B/21